*Twayne's United States Authors Series*

EDITOR OF THIS VOLUME

Sylvia E. Bowman

*Indiana University*

*Thomas Paine*

TUSAS 301

Thomas Paine, 1792
Engraving by Sharp of portrait by George Romney

# THOMAS PAINE

By JEROME D. WILSON
*Lander College*
and
WILLIAM F. RICKETSON
*Lander College*

TWAYNE PUBLISHERS
A DIVISION OF G. K. HALL & CO., BOSTON

**Library of Congress Cataloging in Publication Data**

Wilson, Jerome D
  Thomas Paine.

  (Twayne's United States authors series ; TUSAS 301)
  Bibliography: p. 162–67.
  Includes index.
  1. Paine, Thomas, 1737–1809. 2. Political
scientists—United States—Biography. 3. Revolution-
ists—United States—Biography. I. Ricketson,
William F., joint author.
JC178.V2W56       320.5'1'0924 [B]        77–15478
ISBN  0–8057–7206–5

# *Contents*

# *About the Authors*

Jerome D. Wilson joined the Lander College faculty in 1973 and is currently Associate Professor and Chairman of the Department of Humanities. A native of South Carolina, he received his undergraduate education at the University of South Carolina, the Master's degree from Appalachian State University, and the Ph.D. from Auburn University. Having a special interest in the American Colonial and Early National periods, Professor Wilson has published several articles on Thomas Paine, including an annotated bibliography and a study of Paine's relationship with the early South Carolina figures Henry and John Laurens.

William F. Ricketson has been a member of the history faculty at Lander College since 1967 and has been Professor of History and Chairman of the Social Sciences Department since 1973. He received the baccalaureate degree from Mercer University, the M.Div. and the Th.M. degrees from Southern Baptist Theological Seminary, and the M.A. degree from the University of North Carolina. Professor Ricketson's special interest in the early period of American history began at the University of Georgia, where he received the Ph.D. in 1965. He has published several articles and book reviews on topics pertaining to the Colonial and Revolutionary periods of American history.

# *Preface*

Tom Paine — the name is still likely to call forth differing images: a wild-eyed radical delighting in the destruction wrought by violent revolution; an unrepentant sinner who grasped a bottle and berated the Bible with his final breaths; a generous spirit who labored tirelessly during his long life in the cause of personal freedom. Each of these views has in the century and a half since Paine's death been espoused by one group or another; and, while each view has some truth in it, no one category presents the true Thomas Paine.

Paine was a rebel, a revolutionist; he was also a propagandist par excellence, a mover of men's minds — and perhaps the most effective writer of persuasive literature in the history of the English language. And it is as a writer that we wish to deal with Paine, for to know his writing is to understand better the origins of the republican form of government in the Western world, to know why we exalt the worth of the common man, and why we continue to guard zealously the individual's right to "life, liberty, and the pursuit of happiness."

While a definitive study of Paine is beyond the scope of this book, certain key questions must be answered if we are to understand this complex man who has for more than a century been the object of acclaim, controversy, and denunciation. Concerning the American phase of Paine's career, we must examine closely his involvement with the movement for independence: How well did Paine really understand the character of the American Revolution? In dealing with the second phase of his career, we must investigate the backgrounds of eighteenth-century rationalism in order to see clearly why Paine, who was so successful in inciting revolution in America, failed so miserably in England: How deep was his understanding of Hobbesian metaphysics and Lockean philosophy? The third phase of Paine's literary-political career saw the production of the controversial and inflammatory *Age of Reason,* which set forth his views on religion: How important is this work in a modern assessment of Paine?

While Paine may be accurately thought of as a true son of the eighteenth-century Enlightenment, he was more of an individualist than many of his contemporaries. Paine and the *philosophes* share two major elements of commonality: both were influenced by René Descartes in philosophy and by Sir Isaac Newton in science, and both translated the new rationalism into the language of the common man. However, in the areas of politics — where he made his greatest contribution — Paine, more than any of the *philosophes,* made a clean break with the past when he advocated the feasibility of republicanism. We shall examine the influence, or lack of influence, of such thinkers as Descartes, Newton, Locke, Diderot, and Rousseau upon Paine; and, in conclusion, emphasize Paine's characteristic individuality as the great strength of his writing.

A new and more objective appraisal of Paine as a figure who made significant contributions to Western institutions also seems called for at the present time, for recent historical scholarship has, on the one hand, led us to view Paine as contributing to a less monolithic view of eighteenth-century revolution, and biblical scholarship has, on the other hand, verified much of what in times past seemed to be his defamation of the Scriptures. In view of such changes, the time is appropriate for a critical-analytical study — the first such to be made of Paine's writings.

# Acknowledgments

We wish to express gratitude to Citadel Press for allowing us permission to quote from *The Complete Writings of Thomas Paine* and to the F. W. Faxon Company for permission to reproduce material from *The Bulletin of Bibliography*. Special thanks also go to Mrs. L. B. Adams for so graciously making available to us her rare volumes of Paine's writings and to Professor Robert D. Little, of Western Carolina University, who read portions of the manuscript and offered invaluable suggestions.

# Chronology

1737    Thomas Paine born January 29 in Thetford, Norfolk, England, to Joseph and Frances Cocke Paine.

1750    Apprenticed to father to learn trade of staymaking.

1753    Tries to run away to sea.

1757    Practices trade of staymaking in a London shop and attends lectures about Newtonian astronomy.

1759    Opens shop as master staymaker in town of Sandwich, Kent. Marries Mary Lambert, who dies a year later.

1762    Enters customs service as unattached officer (gauger of brewers' casks).

1764    Receives appointment as officer of customs

1765    Dismissed from position (August) for attempting to organize customs officers.

1766    In London, teaches English at an academy operated by Noble.

1768    Reappointed to excise service, district of Lewes, Sussex.

1771    Marries Elizabeth Ollive (March), daughter of a tradesman.

1772-    Writes *Case of the Officers of Excise,* his earliest known
1773    prose composition and first important pamphlet. Solicits Oliver Goldsmith's aid in getting cause of excisemen before Parliament.

1774    Discharged from excise service. Secures legal separation from wife. Arrives in America (November 30); bears letter of introduction from Benjamin Franklin.

1775    Becomes editor of Robert Aitken's *Pennsylvania Magazine.* Publishes anti-slavery essay, *African Slavery in America.* Anticipates Declaration of Independence in *A Serious Thought.*

1777    Writes *Common Sense* (January). Enlists and serves as aide-de-camp to General Nathanael Greene and sees action at Fort Lee. Publishes *The Forester's Letters* (April-May) and expands *Common Sense.* Produces *Crisis* I.

1777    Writes *Crisis* II and III. Appointed secretary to the commissioners for an Indian treaty. Congressional appointment as Secretary to Committee on Foreign Affairs for the Congress. *Crisis* IV ("Sept. 12 at noon").

1778   Produces *Crisis* V (March), *Supernumerary* 1 (June), *Crisis* VI (October) and *Crisis* VII (November).

1779   Resigns as foreign affairs secretary as result of Silas Deane affair. Appointed Clerk of Pennsylvania Assembly.

1780   Writes *Crisis* VIII (February) and IX (June). University of Pennsylvania confers honorary degree. Publishes *Crisis Extraordinary* and *Public Good,* which refutes Virginia's claims to Western lands. Contributed three hundred dollars toward establishment of Bank of Pennsylvania.

1781   Accompanies Colonel John Laurens to France on diplomatic mission.

1782   Publishes *Crisis* X (March) and XI (May), *Supernumerary Crisis* (June), *Letter to the Abbé Raynal,* and *Crisis* XII (October).

1783   *Crisis* XIII (April) and *A Supernumerary Crisis* (December).

1784   State of New York presents him with farm at New Rochelle.

1785   Designs single-arch bridge; invents smokeless candle.

1786   Writes *Dissertations on Government; the Affairs of the Bank; and Paper Money,* supporting the Bank of North America.

1787   Takes bridge proposal to France to submit to French Academy of Sciences. Writes *Prospects on the Rubicon.*

1788   Returns to England to promote bridge. Meets Charles Fox, Lord Landsdowne, Edmund Burke.

1790   Receives key to Bastille from the Marquis de Lafayette for presentation to George Washington.

1791   Publishes *Rights of Man,* part I. Denounces king and monarchy in *A Republican Manifesto.*

1792   Writes second part of *Rights of Man* and *Letter Addressed to Addressers.* Embarks again for France to take seat in National Assembly. Charged with sedition; tried in absentia; found guilty of treason.

1793   Addresses National Convention, urging banishment, not death, of Louis XVI. Writes *The Age of Reason,* part I. Arrested and imprisoned by French.

1794   Intercession of James Monroe secures release from prison. Returns to Convention.

1795 Publishes *Dissertation on the First Principles of Government* and *The Age of Reason,* part II.
1796 Writes *Agrarian Justice, The Decline and Fall of the English System of Finance,* and *Letter to George Washington.*
1802 Returns to America. Contributes numerous letters to newspapers.
1806 Suffers a light stroke.
1807 Writes *Examination of the Prophecies,* last published work. Makes his will.
1809 Dies June 8. Buried on New Rochelle farm.

CHAPTER 1

# Markings: Youth and Manhood
# in England

*Sweet smiling village, loveliest of the lawn,*
*Thy sports are fled, and all thy charms withdrawn;*
*Amidst thy bowers the tyrant's hand is seen,*
*And desolation saddens all thy green.*

WHEN Oliver Goldsmith penned "The Deserted Village" in
1770, he did not pattern "sweet Auburn" on any actual
English village; but Thomas Paine, reading it for the first time,
might well have thought the author had done so. Certainly the
resemblances between the poet's "loveliest village" and Paine's
own Thetford were many. Like Auburn, Thetford had seen her
small yeoman farmers displaced and forced into cities by the
encroachments of the Enclosure Acts; she had seen her lower
classes increasingly victimized by harsh laws and aristocratic
inequalities; she had seen her town corporation become corruption
ridden and her people seemingly powerless to effect a change; she
had seen the traditional, centuries-old ways of life disappear as the
nation gradually shifted from an agricultural to an industrial
economy.

Paine, restive at the age of thirty-three, his youth behind him and
his future uncertain, would have been deeply stirred and his
smoldering resentment would have been fuelled by Goldsmith's
moving indictment of the "new age of tyranny of trade, material
luxury and pride."[1] Something — we can fancifully suppose that it
might have been this sentimental poem — suddenly fused Paine's
fragmented capabilities and frustrations; for he resolved for the
first time to dip pen in ink in support of a cause. With that pen-

stroke Paine embarked on a career which was to change the course
of nations and ultimately earn him the esteem of people everywhere
who cherish republican principles.

## I   *The Thetford Years*

Although both Paine and Cocke were old and distinguished
names in the history of Norfolk County, Frances Cocke Paine was
considered to be socially superior to her husband, for she was
Church of England and the daughter of a Thetford attorney.
Eleven years younger than his wife, Joseph Paine was a sober and
industrious townsman who plied the trade of staymaking, tilled a
small plot of ground in his spare hours, and rigorously followed the
teachings of the Quakers, the only dissenting religious sect in Thetford. At that time, the town had some two thousand inhabitants
and was a posting center on the main road to London.

The son, Thomas, who was born to the Paines on January 29,
1737, spent his early years in the plain brick house on Bridge Street.
Though he never formally joined the Society of Friends and was, in
fact, said to have been confirmed in the Church of England,[2] many
critics have felt that the Quaker meetings he attended as a child
exerted a far greater influence upon Paine than did the Anglican
Church. Moncure D. Conway, one of Paine's important biographers, has maintained that the small Quaker meetinghouse on Cage
Lane "was his more important birthplace,"[3] and designated
Quakerism as the single most important source for Paine's religious
ideas and for many of his political ones. While some readers have
cautioned against placing undue stress on the Quaker background,
it seems plausible to conclude, with R. R. Palmer, that it was
"probably from his Quaker elders that Paine first acquired his dis-
tinctive habits of mind, in particular his humanitarian aversion to
cruelty and his bold faith in his own judgments."[4] Certainly Paine,
like his Quaker forebears, placed little or no importance on established traditions, class rank, and economic status.

Although Paine attended the local grammar school as a boy, he
did not learn Latin, one of the standard subjects taught in schools
at that time. Writing of his youth many years later, he explained: "I
did not learn Latin ... because of the objection the Quakers have
against the books in which the language is taught."[5] Here again we
must pause to consider briefly a problem that has occupied the

attention of Paine scholars from time to time: Was Paine, who admittedly "had no inclination to learn languages,"[6] really anti-classical? After a careful examination of Paine's writings, Professor A. O. Aldridge has concluded that he had "absolutely no reverence for antiquity or for the artistic masterpieces of Greece and Rome," That Paine received no inspiration from the Classical tradition, and that he regarded Greek and Latin as useless ornaments whose study only hindered the development of science and enlightenment.[7]

While Aldridge is correct in asserting that Paine showed no reverence for the Classics, we should not lose sight of the fact that Paine, one of the world's truly great practitioners of the art of persuasive writing, did indeed owe a debt of a kind to the Classical tradition; for, when he wrote such highly effective deliberative discourses as *Common Sense* and the *Crisis* papers; he followed very closely the rules prescribed by the Classical rhetoricians. And, though he did not learn Greek and Latin, he must have had some acquaintance with the rhetorical precepts found in Aristotle, Cicero, and Quintilian — Classical authors who would have been studied in some detail in the Thetford grammar school.[8]

Paine's formal education terminated at the age of thirteen when his father removed him from school in order to teach him the trade of staymaking. Paine's biographers have traditionally regarded the elder Paine as a maker of women's corsets, which were known as "stays" because of the rigid bone or metal strips used for stiffening the fabric. Ralph C. Roper, however, believes that Paine was a maker not of corsets but of ship stays (heavy ropes used to brace masts or spars). "Thetford," he claims, "was alive with fishermen and fishing boats, and one of the main occupations was the making of ship stays."[9] Whether cables or corsets, young Paine learned to make them; and he followed the trade of staymaking sporadically for the next ten years.

During his few years of schooling, Paine's appetite for adventure had been whetted by tales of service on a man-of-war which he had heard from William Knowle, one of the teachers with whom he had become friends. So, tired of the confining trade that he plied, Paine, at the age of seventeen, signed on as crewman of the privateer *Terrible,* under the command of a certain Captain Death. He writes that "from this adventure I was happily prevented by the affectionate and moral remonstrance of a good father."[10] And it

was well for him his father had intervened, for less than a year later
the *Terrible,* engaged in a disastrous sea battle, lost three-fourths of
its two-hundred-man crew. Paine was not to be deterred from a sea
venture, however, and in 1756, when his father's "moral remonstrance" was very nearly worn away, he signed on another privateer, the *King of Prussia,* and went to sea. It is not known how long
this voyage lasted, but no record exists of his returning to Thetford
until some years later.

## II   *The Curious Staymaker*

Following his stint of sea service, Paine became a staymaker in
the London firm of a Mr. Morris. An important period in Paine's
life, these two London years saw him bent over the workbench by
day; but he was also eating sparely and wearing a threadbare coat
in order to indulge during his after hours in his lifelong penchant
for science. "The natural bent of my mind was to science," Paine
writes, and "as soon as I was able I purchased a pair of globes, and
attended the philosophical lectures of Martin and Ferguson, and
became afterward acquainted with Dr. Bevis, of the society called
the Royal Society, then living in the Temple, and an excellent
astronomer." Benjamin Martin, a mathematician and instrument
maker, and James Ferguson, an astronomer, were disciples of
Newton; and, by means of public lectures, they dispensed a highly
palatable form of the Newtonian doctrine of cosmic harmony and
order. Ferguson had only recently published *Astronomy Explained
on Sir Isaac Newton's Principles* (1756), a manual which explained
astronomical phenomena in such clear and familiar fashion that it
went through thirteen editions by 1811.[12] Though Paine had perhaps read Newton's *Principia* in translation, the popular lectures of
Ferguson and Martin, with their ingenious machines and diagrams,
served to convince him of the essential rightness of the Newtonian
view "that God revealed himself in a creation which was ordered by
a vast hierarchy of immutable laws by which all things operated in
harmony."[13] Some critics, like the late Harry Hayden Clark, have
maintained that the scientific Deism, as put forward by the popularizers of Newtonianism, formed the basis of Paine's later theories
of religion, politics, economics, social service, and education.[14]

### III   *A New Career Beckons*

Following the London interval, Paine moved to Dover. A year later, in 1759, he established himself as a master staymaker in Sandwich, Kent; and, in the same year, he met and married Mary Lambert, an orphaned waiting-woman to the wife of a local woolen draper. When Paine's business did not prosper in this location, he moved to Margate, where his young wife died, possibly in childbirth. Unable to make a satisfactory living at Staymaking, Paine, with his father's approval, abandoned the trade and prepared himself for the excise service, a branch of government service similar to our present-day customs service. According to Conway, he returned to Thetford in 1761, where, "acting as a supernumerary officer of excise, he continued his studies ... [and] on December 1, 1762, he was appointed to gauge brewers' casks at Grantham. On August 8, 1764, he was set to watch smugglers at Alford."[15]

Paine could hardly have chosen an occupation better calculated to enhance his unpopularity or to ensure his continued low fortune than the excise service. For not only were the excise acts distasteful — "odious to the people," Conway reports — but the officers had also become negligent and the service itself corrupt. Smuggling was so widespread that, by 1748, some twelve thousand persons had been convicted for offenses against the act which levied a tax of one pound on every gallon of liquor.[16] Moreover, the post was not without danger, for the lone outriding officer who apprehended a band of smugglers on some lonely inlet placed his very life in jeopardy. Such hazard was hardly compensated for in salary; for, out of the fifty pounds which Paine received annually, he had to keep his horse as well as himself. It is not very surprising, therefore, to learn of Paine's dismissal from the service in 1765 for "stamping" — entering in his books examinations which had not actually been made — that was a practice by no means uncommon among the harried and underpaid officers.

After returning briefly to staymaking, Paine tried teaching English in an academy run by a Mr. Noble. Early in 1766 he wrote an apologetic letter to the excise board requisting reinstatement, and on July 11 his restoration was granted, though no place could be found for him in the service at that time. He continued to teach until February 1768, when he received an appointment as officer at

Lewes, Sussex. It was here that Paine first met Thomas "Clio" Rickman, who was to furnish encouragement and shelter during many troubled times ahead and who was later to become his biographer.

Rickman describes Paine at this time as "notorious for that quality which has been defined perseverance in a good cause and obstinacy in a bad one. He was tenacious of his opinions, which were bold, acute, and independent, and which he maintained with ardour, elegance, and argument."[17] Love of argument — which was to be Paine's forte in America — drew him to join a local social club which met evenings at the White Hart tavern. Here he soon gained the reputation as the most dogged and persistent of debaters, becoming virtual custodian of the old Greek Homer which was sent the morning after a meeting to the most obstinate haranguer in the previous evening's debate. Rickman tells us that Paine won the book so often it was given the title "'The Headstrong Book, or Original Book of Obstinacy.' Written by ***** ****, of Lewes, in Sussex, and Revised and Corrected by THOMAS PAINE."[18]

In 1771, Paine remarried. Ten years his junior, Elizabeth Ollive was the daughter of a small tobacco-shop owner, Samuel Ollive, with whom Paine had lodged during his first year at Lewes. When Ollive died in 1769, Paine had moved out; but he had aided the impoverished widow and daughter in opening up a small grocer's shop. Having a Quaker background, Elizabeth was disposed to look favorably on Paine's proposal; and, after the marriage, he resumed his former residence at the Ollive home.

While at Lewes, Paine's spreading reputation as an "outspoken and dogmatic champion of unpopular causes"[19] led to his active involvement in the cause of the excise officers, who at last were uniting to obtain a raise in pay. Chosen to draw up a statement of grievances, Paine produced his first important pamphlet, *Case of the Officers of Excise,* which was printed for distribution to members of Parliament and to others who might be favorable to the cause. In the plain and forthright style that became the hallmark of Paine's later and more famous writings, he argued the case of the excisemen concisely, yet vigorously and convincingly. As Conway notes, "there was, of course, no room for originality in the simple task of showing that the ill-paid service must be badly done, but the style is remarkable for simplicity and force."[20]

Following a brief introduction, Paine developed his argument in three sections: part one, which concerns the state of the salary, enumerates the many ills attendant upon the low pay; part two considers the corruption of principles and temptations to dishonesty to which poverty gives rise; part three discusses arguments, restates the purpose, and finally envisions a rejuvenated service in which the financial cure "would be as extensive as the complaint, and new health out-root the present corruption."[21]

While this short work is not sufficiently important to merit a detailed investigation, it is in one sense portentous; for it displays that same force and logic that would do so much to move a vacillating America to action a few years hence. The absence of jargon and learned terms, the coined phrases designed to stick in the mind ("Poor and in poverty are powerful temptations"), the skillful use of devices like repetition of key ideas and carefully framed rhetorical questions, the concrete diction and clearly articulated sentences, the carefully modulated ethical appeal implicit in the whole work — these qualities mark *Case of the Officers of Excise* as the work of a journeyman propagandist — as an apprentice but as one who needs only to hone his tools and refine his technique in order to become a master of the art of persuasive writing.

Using the five hundred pounds which the excisemen had raised, Paine spent the winter of 1772–73 in London trying to get the case before Parliament. By way of letter, he presented Oliver Goldsmith, one of the most popular and widely read authors of the day, a copy of the pamphlet. Paine introduced himself as the "principal promoter of a plan for applying to Parliament this session for an increase in salary"[22] and concluded by asking to meet Goldsmith. While there is no proof that, as Philip Foner maintains, "Goldsmith replied to this letter and he and Paine became very close friends,"[23] we do know that the two men did meet.

When, in spite of his best efforts, Parliament refused to hear the case, Paine returned to Lewes. His agitating activities having directed the unfavorable attention of his superiors toward him, Paine received in April 1774 official notification of his dismissal from the service for "having quitted his business, without obtaining the Board's Leave for so doing, and being gone off on Account of the Debts which he hath contracted...."[24] When Paine again petitioned the board for reinstatement, his appeal was rejected.

To make matters worse, Paine's wife had not been able to show a profit from the grocer shop; and, in danger of arrest for debt, he was forced to sell the stock and furniture — even the tobacco mill — in order to satisfy the creditors. In June, the Paines separated; and an air of mystery surrounds their separation, for neither party would ever discuss it. When questioned about it by Rickman, Paine replied: "It is nobody's business but my own; I had cause for it, but I will name it to no one."[25] Crane Brinton has suggested that the separation was due, "not to any scandal, but to temperamental difficulties on both sides."[26] Whatever the cause, both parties signed the articles of separation, and Paine surrendered all rights to the property his wife had brought him.

## IV   *America on the Horizon*

So, at the age of thirty-seven, penniless but free of marital and financial responsibilities, Paine once again turned toward London. While Conway, the most complete chronicler of Paine's early life, records very little of his activities during the months prior to his departure for America, Aldridge surmises that he "indulged his interest in politics and science"[27] and perhaps eked out a living by returning to his old trade of staymaking. By some means, perhaps through the agency of excise board member George Lewis Scott, he met Benjamin Franklin, then serving as colonial agent in England. It could have been their shared interest in science which induced the good-natured Franklin to take an interest in Paine — or was it the latent revolutionary that the astute Dr. Franklin perceived? At any rate, when Paine made known his desire to try his luck in America, Franklin was sufficiently impressed to give him a letter of introduction to Richard Bache, his son-in-law. Dated September 30, 1774, the letter reads:

The bearer, Mr. Thomas Paine, is very well recommended to me, as an ingenious, worthy young man. He goes to Pennsylvania with a view of settling there.

I request you to give him your best advice and countenance, as he is quite a stranger there. If you can put him in a way of obtaining employment as a clerk, or assistant tutor in a school, or assistant surveyor, (of all which I think him very capable), so that he may procure a subsistence at least, till he can make acquaintance and obtain a knowledge of the country, you will do well, and much oblige your affectionate father. My love to Sally and the boys.

B. Franklin[28]

Early in October, the "ingenious, worthy young man," possessing little more than Franklin's letter and a good deal of determination, boarded the *London Packet,* which was bound for Philadelphia. As the shores of his homeland receded into the graying distance, Paine resolutely put behind him half a lifetime of failure and frustration. Looking beyond the horizon to the New World, he could not have known that he was on the threshold of tumultuous events which not only would involve him directly but would also change his life and the lives of generations yet unborn.

CHAPTER 2

# Times to Try Men's Souls

IN order to understand the events in which Paine became embroiled soon after his arrival in Philadelphia, we should not forget the unique position which America occupied in the family of the British Empire. She was an English possession; and, according to the prevailing theory of mercantilism, she existed for the benefit of the mother country. These colonies were, however, unusual; for, separated from mother-England by a vast expanse of ocean, daughter-America had exercised a marked degree of self-government and had grown prosperous during a period of "salutary neglect" while England was preoccupied with the Seven Years War. But, when peace came in 1763, the conditions that affected the colonies abruptly changed. Staggering under an enormous war debt, England attempted to raise revenue in her possessions by imposing certain taxes. While these were not oppressive measures, as taxes go, the colonists feared, as T. A. Bailey put it, that, "if they were forced to pay one penny, they might one day have to pay their last penny."[1] Raising a cry of "taxation without representation," they began a course of resistance that was to climax ten years later in the fateful "shot heard round the world"[2] on April 19, 1775.

While Paine was still tossing upon the stormy North Atlantic, George III was writing to Prime Minister Lord North that "the New England governments are in a state of rebellion, blows must decide whether they are to be subject to this country or independent."[3] The decision to come to blows was the king's own; it was not one which the colonists, recalcitrant though they were, would have made. Few of the two-and-a-half million Americans scattered along the Eastern Seabord in 1774 actually desired to separate from Great Britain. Even as late as May 1775, George Washington declared to the Reverend Jonathan Boucher that, "If you ever hear of my joining in any such measures, you have my leave to set me down for everything wicked."[4] While the colonials were restive and protested — sometimes in a rather violent fashion, it is true — what they regarded as infringements of their "rights" by the British, there was not in the decade preceding 1775 any concerted move afoot to separate from the Empire and to establish an independent American nation. Though some voices could be heard advocating independence, they were heard covertly and singly, not in unison. And even after Lexington and Concord had made separation inevitable, many Americans continued to hope for reconciliation.

## I   *A Crusading Editor*

Paine arrived in America a desperately ill man. Suffering from the "putrid fever" (probably typhus) which had ravaged the *London Packet* during the nine-week passage, Paine was so weakened when the boat docked at Philadelphia on November 30, 1774, that he was even unable to turn himself in bed. Fortunately, word spread that he carried letters of introduction from Dr. Franklin, and friends of the great Philadelphian carried Paine ashore and cared for him until his strength returned. By March 1775, Paine wrote to Franklin that ". . . a printer and Bookseller here, a man of reputation, and property, a Robert Aitken, has lately attempted a magazine, but having little or no turn that way himself, has applied to me for assistance. He had not above 600 subscribers when I first assisted him. We have now upwards of 1500 and daily increasing."[5] Aitken had been so impressed with Paine's contribution to the first issue of his *Pennsylvania Magazine* that he had offered him the position of editor of the fledgling journal. That Paine was suited to the task is shown by the swelling subscription list. As Gorham Munson has noted, here was "the first real opportunity for Paine's writing talent to burgeon,"[6] and he brought to this work the same intensity and unflagging zeal which were to characterize his dedication in the years ahead to the cause of revolution in America, England, and France.

Much of the material with which Paine filled the pages of the magazine during his months as crusading editor was written by him, but he signed the pieces with pseudonyms like "Vox Pupuli," "Atlanticus," or "Humanus."[7] Broadly speaking, these writings fall into three categories: 1. attempts at "Fine" writing (poems and essays written primarily to entertain) and informative or instructive articles; 2. pieces which plead some humanitarian cause; 3. essays and poems whose political messages foreshadow *Common Sense.*

Inspired by a collection of minerals displayed at the Philadelphia Library Company, "Useful and Entertaining Hints," Paine's first essay, for the February 1775 number, exemplifies those pieces in the first grouping which strain for a conscious elegance and "literary" quality. Eschewing the plain style of the excise pamphlet, Paine speculates about America's hidden mineral resources in a series of paragraphs marked by their Latinate diction and by elaborate sentence patterns in which the parts are too obviously balanced, paralleled, and antithesized. The heavy-handed rhetorical flourishes serve rather to amuse than to entertain — for example, Paine's labored allusion to nature as an antiquated beauty who "locks and bolts up her private recesses with extraordinary care" (II, 1024). Similarly, in "Reflections on the Life and Death of Lord Clive," which Aldridge has assessed as "more like bad poetry than good prose,"[8] we can almost see Paine strike the pose as he apostrophizes: "Oh, India! thou loud proclaimer of European cruelties, thou bloody monument of unnecessary deaths, be tender in the day of enquiry, and show a Christian world thou canst suffer and forgive" (II, 23). Happily, Paine soon abandoned such a pretentious style and resumed his plain and forthright manner of composition for such informative articles as "Description of a New Electrical Machine" and "A New Method of Building Frame Houses."

More numerous are the writings of this year which give some glimpse of Paine the humanitarian. Appalled at the half-million slaves in the colonies, Paine wrote an antislavery essay, "African Slavery in America," shortly after he arrived, though it was not published until early March. Aside from bringing Paine the acquaintance of Dr. Benjamin Rush, that eminent colonist who was waging a campaign against both slavery and British domination, this "early manifesto of abolitionism," as Conway termed it, gave added impetus to the growing antislavery movement, for the first American society for the abolition of slavery was formed in Philadelphia less than a month after its publication. Paine's tract was not, however, the first denunciation of slavery to be printed in America, as many of his more ardent admirers have claimed. Thomas Jefferson had called for emancipation of slaves in Virginia as early as 1769, and Samuel Sewall had written against it in New England much earlier than that.

Aside from countering the arguments of those who maintained that the Scriptures sanctioned slavery, Paine farsightedly looks beyond the act of abolition to consider the methods by which the body of newly freed slaves might be accommodated within the existing framework of society. The old and infirm, he conjectures, should be cared for by their former owners, "who enjoyed the labor of their better days"; for the rest, "prudent men, with the assistance of legislatures" (II, 17, 19) would decide what would be practicable and best.

In referring several times to the "natural rights" of those enslaved, Paine touches upon a theme that he developed more fully in *Common Sense* and that he later established as the philosophical credo of *Rights of Man,* the maturest expression of his political philosophy. While his Quaker antecedents might, in part, be responsible for his humanitarian desire to eradicate the stain of slavery, the "light of nature," as Paine perceived it, that had filtered down from John Locke and Sir Isaac Newton can be isolated as a more important factor in his equalitarian outlook, even at this early point in his journalistic career. The idea — which is merely foreshadowed — that every individual has a birthright of freedom, that such birthright is the "natural, perfect right of all mankind" (II, 19), would in subsequent writings strike the tenor of the whole.

Known today as one of history's great egalitarians, Paine demonstrated in many of these early essays his disdain for earthly pomp and power and his strong convictions in the matter of equal rights. In his brief allegorical vision, "New Anecdotes of Alexander the Great," for instance, the persona recounts a visit to the Plutonian world where he encounters the mightly Alexander, who is transformed first into a horse and then into a bug. Since he is "a most contemptible figure of the downfall of tyrant greatness," the narrator contemptuously suffers him to "nibble on a pimple that was newly risen on my hand, in order to refresh him" (II, 1114–15).

In a similar short allegory, "Cupid and Hymen," Paine recounts the story of Cupid's interference in the plans of a lecherous — but rich — old lord to wed a luckless peasant girl; and the purpose of his narrative is to expose the unfortunate consequences of a loveless union. In "Reflections on Unhappy Marriages," Paine again deplores marriages made for money; and he wryly observes that, of

Christian — church — sanctioned unions, "not one in a hundred of them had anything to do either with happiness or common sense." The felicitous Indian marriages demanded, however, "no other ceremony than mutual affection, and last no longer than they bestow mutual pleasures" (II, 1120). These views on marriage and divorce, needless to say, were far ahead of their time.

In other pieces Paine exposed the ridiculousness of the custom of duelling, attacked inhumane treatment of animals, pled for national and international copyright laws, and disparaged the bestowing of titles. In fact, few instances of man's inhumanity to man that moved within his ken during this journalistic phase of his career escaped being preserved in a specimen essay published somewhere in the pages of the *Pennsylvania Magazine*.[9]

In looking through these diverse writings of Paine's first year in America, it is clear that from the outset he harbored no illusions that Parliament would redress colonial grievances and that he began, soon after he assumed his editorial duties, to wage a not very subtle campaign for separation from Great Britain. Indeed, even before he took the editor's chair he defended the Americans' position, though in a tempered fashion, in the form of an imaginary dialogue between the ghost of General Wolfe, killed during the attack on Quebec in 1759, and General Gage, the last British governor of Massachusetts. In the dialogue, printed January 4, 1775, Wolfe, at the insistence of a group of British heroes, has returned to the world of the living to try to open the eyes of Gage to the dirty business he is engaged in — a business "unworthy of a British soldier and a freeman." "You have come here," Wolfe upbraids him, "to deprive your fellow citizens of their liberty" (II, 47–48). When Gage remonstrates that he is merely following orders, Wolfe declares that, as British subjects, the colonists have been deprived of the essence of liberty, for they are no longer free to choose their own rulers.

In an introductory essay as editor, in a piece written in January 1775, and entitled "The Magazine in America," Paine spoke of America as having "now outgrown her infancy ... while proud antiquity, like a skeleton in rags, parades the streets of other nations, their genius, as if sickened and disgusted with the phantom, comes hither for recovery" (II, 1109). In May, scarcely a month after the battle of Lexington, Paine published "The Dream Interpreted," in which he used the literary format of the dream vision to bring home his political message. In this short narrative, the dreamer tells the reader that he found himself in his dream in "one of the most pleasing landscapes I have ever beheld" (II, 50); for he was surrounded by fruiting trees and sparkling rivers. But, as he gazed at this tranquil place, the sun began to burn the land, the vegetation to wither, and then the sky to darken with an approaching storm. At length the storm broke, with lightning so fierce that "a general discharge of the whole artillery of heaven was poured down upon the earth." When the fury abated, however, the prospect was again "lovely and inviting, and had all the appearance of exceeding its former glory" (II, 51). Not trusting the reader to make the connection for himself, Paine has the dreamer encounter a traveller who "interprets" the dream. "That beautiful country which you saw is America," he tells the dreamer. "The sickly state you beheld her in has been coming on her for these ten years past.... The tempest is the present contest, and the event will be the same. She will rise with new glories from the conflict, and her fame will be established in every corner of the globe (II, 52).

Following Bunker Hill, Paine published in July a short piece, "Thoughts on Defensive War," in which he explained why he could not subscribe to the pacifism of the Quakers. He exhorts the colonists to take up arms because their unprincipled enemy can be brought to reason and moderation only by arms or miracles. "While a single nation refuses to lay them down," he writes, "it is proper that all should keep them up"; for arms, like laws, "discourage and keep the invader and plunderer in awe, and preserve order in the world as well as property" (II, 53). In fact, he concludes that "the lives of hundreds in both countries would have been preserved had America been in arms a year ago" (II, 55).

When the king formally declared in August that the colonies were in a state of rebellion, Paine answered with a stirring song, "Liberty Tree," whose last stanza, as Foner has noted, was a definite forecast of *Common Sense;* for Paine emphasized that "Kings, Commons, and Lords" were the "tyrannical powers" which were united to cut down the tree of liberty (II, 1091n, 1092). And a month later, in October, writing once again on the topic of Negro slavery in "A Serious Thought," Paine, who reflects on the "horrid cruelties exercised by Britain," "hesitate[s] not for a moment to believe that the Almighty will finally separate America from

Britain" (II, 20). Professor D. S. Muzzey has called this short tract "the first plea for independence published in America."[10]

## II  *Our First Best-Seller*

"Have you seen the pamphlet 'Common Sense'?" wrote Charles Lee to General Washington. "I never saw such a masterly, irresistible performance.... I own myself convinced by the arguments, of the necessity of separation."[11] General Lee's reaction is a typical one, for Paine's latest pamphlet, his most ambitious literary undertaking to date, was literally taking the country by storm. *Common Sense* made its appearance in Philadelphia on January 10, 1776, the same day that news of the king's bellicose speech to Parliament was received. Paine later confided to Henry Laurens, president of the Continental Congress, that he was so sure of the British reaction to the Congress's latest petition that he had contrived to have the pamphlet come out "just at the time the [king's] speech might arrive in America, and so fortunate was I in this cast of policy that both of them made their appearance in this city on the same day" (II, 1162).

Although Paine had originally intended to publish *Common Sense* as a series of newspaper letters, he could find no editor bold enough to print such inflammatory work. Dr. Rush, who had read the manuscript and had suggested the title, directed him to Robert Bell, an outspoken Scottish printer, who agreed to print it if Paine would bear any loss that might be incurred. The terms called for Bell to receive half of the profits and to set aside the other half for the purchase of mittens for the colonial troops going to Quebec. Priced at two shillings, the first printing of a thousand copies sold out within days. It was a "success that probably astonished even Paine himself," comments Nelson Adkins.[12] A second edition with "Large Additions" was hastily prepared and offered for sale on January 20. So unprecedented was the demand for the pamphlet that Paine then enlarged it by one-third by adding an appendix and an address to the Quakers, and had six thousand copies printed at his own expense. By March it had sold 120,000 copies, "the greatest sale that any performance ever had since the use of letters," wrote Paine with his characteristic lack of modesty (II, 1163). In all, the pamphlet had nineteen editions in the colonies, seven in Great Britain, and had a French translation published in Rotterdam. In spite of its tremendous sale, however, Paine received none of the financial rewards; he gave the copyright to every state in the union and his share of the profits to the war effort. In fact, he complained in 1779 that he was still thirty-nine pounds "out of pocket" to an unscrupulous publisher.

The pamphlet, which had been published anonymously, was variously attributed to Franklin, to Samuel Adams, and to John Adams. The latter Adams heard himself introduced in France as *"le fameux Adams,* author of *Common Sense."*[13] When Franklin was reproached by a British lady for referring to the king as "the royal brute of Great Britain," he hastened to assure her that he had not written *Common Sense* and, furthermore, that he would never so have dishonored the brute creation.[14]

A brief look at some of the opinions of Paine's contemporaries indicates the decided effect that the pamphlet was having. The day after he received General Lee's letter, Washington wrote to Joseph Reed: "A few more such flaming arguments, as were exhibited at Falmouth and Norfolk, added to the sound doctrine and unanswerable reasoning contained in the pamphlet 'Common Sense,' will not leave numbers at a loss to decide upon the propriety of separation."[15] At the begining of March, Abigail Adams confessed to her husband that she was "charmed with the sentiments of 'Common Sense,' . . . and wonder how an honest heart . . . can hesitate one moment at adopting them."[16] Early in April, Washington wrote that he had found the tract "working a purposeful change in the minds of men," and a news writer in New York spoke of it as having "converted thousands to independence that could not endure the idea before."[17] On June 7, 1776, the day on which Richard Henry Lee introduced into Congress his resolutions for independence, William Gordon, the historian of the Revolution, wrote that *"'Common Sense,'* written by Mr. Thomas Paine . . . has produced most astonishing effects, and been received with vast applause, read by almost every American, and recommended as a work replete with truth, and against which none but the partial and prejudiced can form any objections."[18]

Since it was the "first clear, far-carrying appeal for republicanism addressed to American ears,"[19] *Common Sense* deserves rather closer attention than Paine's other writings of the Revolutionary years. The pamphlet is divided into four principal parts, and each is titled to indicate the subject of that section. A short introduction succinctly states the problem (the colonies suffer from "a long and violent abuse of power"), isolates the cause (the king and Parliament), notes the universal nature of the issue ("the cause of America ... is the cause of all mankind"), and lists the charges against the British (destruction of property, infringement of rights, extirpation of those who defend such rights). Paine did not have to contrive an introduction that would arouse interest, for circumstances assured that his subjects would have their own interest for the colonial readers.

In the first division, Paine has a two-fold purpose. First, a series of finely balanced antitheses differentiate the terms "society" and "government": "Society is produced by our wants and government by our wickedness; the former promotes our happiness *positively* by uniting our affections, the latter *negatively* by restraining our vices. The one encourages intercourse; the other creates distinctions. The first is a patron, the last a punisher" (I, 4). "Society," Paine continues, "in every state is a blessing," whereas government, "even in its best state is but a necessary evil" (I, 4).

To gain proper understanding of the design and end of government, he uses an example of a small group of people who settle in some uninhabited part of the earth. By necessity, the colonists come together as a society; then, as the colony grows, they find it necessary to form some type of government to ensure each individual's freedom and security. They deliberate, formulate laws, choose representatives, have elections — and Paine describes the elective process of republican government in some detail. Government, whose design and end is freedom and security, is made necessary, he summarizes, "by the inability of moral virtue to govern the world...," and he concludes that "the simple voice of nature and reason will say it is right" (I, 6.)

Having accounted for the origin of government, Paine moves to his second purpose — an examination of the "so much boasted constitution of England" (I, 6). He brands it as "imperfect, subject to convulsions, incapable of producing what it seems to promise..." While its complexity accounts, in part, for its imperfection, its greatest weakness lies in the fact that its component parts are "the base remains of two ancient tyrannies": the monarchical tyranny in the person of a king, and the aristocratical tyranny in the persons of the peers. Paine derides the idea that the House of Commons acts as a check on the king, for such a check presupposes that the king can't be trusted. On the other hand, Paine reasons, the king can check the Commons; therefore, the constitution "supposes that the king is wiser than those whom it has already supposed to be wiser than him. A mere absurdity!" (I, 7).

An analogy illustrates Paine's assertion that the king is the dominant power in the land. A machine has a series of wheels, all of which are put in motion by one. The entire machine's rate of movement is determined by this one wheel, which the other wheels can slow down but cannot stop. "The first moving power will at last have its way, and what it wants in speed is supplied in time" (I, 8). This single wheel that supplies the motive power is, of course, the crown. Paine concludes his examination by admonishing the people for believing that they have some voice in the government, for "...the will of the king is as much the law of the land in Britain as in France. It is simply handed to the people under the formidable shape of an act of Parliament. For the fate of Charles the First hath only made kings more subtle — not more just" (I, 9).

Taking up the issues of monarchy and hereditary succession, Paine opens part two with the statement that all men were "originally equals in the order of creation." Since there is no natural or religious reason for the distinction of men into kings and subjects, his purpose shall be to inquire "how a race of men came into the world so exalted above the rest . . . and whether they are the means of happiness or of misery to mankind" (I, 9). Since government by kings, he maintains, was first introduced into the world by heathens, from whom the children of Israel copied the custom, it cannot be defended on scriptural authority. As evidence, he offers portions of the Old Testament which deny man the authority to establish earthly kingdoms, a "form of government which so impiously invades the prerogative of heaven" (I, 10). Paine will have no equivocating: "That the Almighty has here entered his protest against monarchical government is true, or the scripture is false" (I, 12).

Paine next turns to denounce that "insult and imposition on posterity" (I, 13), hereditary succession. He asserts, first, that "no one by birth could have a right to set up his own family in perpetual preference to all others forever" (I, 13) and, second, that the electors of a ruler do not have the power to give away the rights of posterity. Paine conjectures that, if we could trace the present race of kings to their origin, we would find the first of them to be "nothing better than the principal ruffian of some restless gang" (I, 13). William the Conqueror, for instance, was but a "French bastard" who landed with a gang of armed men and established himself as king of England against the consent of the natives — "in plain terms a very paltry original" (I, 14).

While the doctrine of hereditary succession is in itself an absurdity, Paine continues, the evil inherent in it concerns mankind. It smacks of oppression in opening a door to "the *foolish,* the *wicked,* and the *improper";* for the public becomes "a prey to every miscreant who can tamper successfully with the follies either of age of infancy" (I, 15). Instead of preserving the nation from civil wars, it serves to promote such conflicts: "in short, monarchy and succession have laid ... but the world in blood and ashes" (I, 16).

In this third and longest of the sections of *Common Sense,* Paine proposes to offer "simple facts, plain arguments, and common sense"; and he asks his reader to "divest himself of prejudice and prepossession and suffer his reason and his feelings to determine for themselves" (I, 17). His overriding purpose — to justify separation and to prompt the hesitant colonists to decisive action — takes on an increasing sense of urgency as the section develops; for Paine implores the reader to forsake the vain hope of reconciliation since "the period of debate is closed [and] arms as a last resource decide the contest" (I, 17).

To prove that not even "the warmest advocate" can show a single advantage to be derived from reconciliation, Paine examines their principal arguments. (a.) A British connection is necessary for America's future happiness. "Nothing can be more fallacious," he retorts. "America would have flourished as much, and probably more, had no European power taken any notice of her" (I, 18). (b.) Britain protected us. Paine responds that her motive was *"interest* and *attachment;* and that she did not protect us from *our enemies on our account;* but from *her enemies* on *her own account"* (I, 18). (c.) Britain is the parent country. "Then the more shame upon her conduct," Paine counters, for "even brutes do not devour their young nor savages make war upon their families" (I, 19). Furthermore, it is Europe, not England, who is the parent country, he argues. (d.) Britain and America united might bid defiance to the world. "Mere presumption," Paine says, for "the fate of war is uncertain." Why should America desire to set the world at defiance anyway, he queries; "our plan is commerce, and that, well attended to, will secure us the peace and friendship of all Europe" (I, 20).

Turning next to the disadvantages of continued union, Paine charts an isolationist course. Alliance with Britain will involve America in European wars and quarrels, he claims; and the best interest of the colonies is to "steer clear of European contentions" (I, 21). Paine regards the great distance at which Britain and America are set apart as added proof that the Almighty never intended the one to have authority over the other, and he cites the fact that the discovery of America preceded the Reformation as evidence that God was preparing a place for Europe's persecuted. Calling up visions of fatherless children, burned houses, and plundered property, Paine exhorts the colonists to shake off the spirit of indecision: "The blood of the slain, the weeping voice of nature cries, 'Tis Time to Part'" (I, 21). Not above resorting to invective, he climaxes his impassioned plea by imploring the Americans not to shrink back and leave the sword to their children, but to reject "the hardened, sullen-tempered Pharaoh of England," to "disdain the wretch, that with the pretended title *Father of His People* can unfeelingly hear of their slaughter, and composedly sleep with their blood upon his soul" (I, 25).

Finally, Paine offers his own plan for a Continental government. He would call a Continental conference for the purpose of framing a constitution, or "Charter of the United Colonies," which would guarantee "freedom and property to all men, and above all things, the free exercise of religion" (I, 29). After outlining in some detail his plan for a representative government, he concludes by reiterating that America's "natural right" is to have a government of her own; for "the last cord is now broken" (I, 30) that has for so long bound her to Britain.

In the fourth part, Paine continues to set forth reasons for immediate separation. He argues that the colonies, now unified and debt free, are able to mount sufficient troop strength to defend the scattered towns and ports. As for the war, it could be paid for by selling the frontier lands, which also would provide revenue for the operation of the new government. Countering the arguments of those who pointed to Britain's superior naval strength, Paine asserts that only a small percentage of the British fleet could be brought to bear against America at any one time. With its natural resources,

America could build and maintain a navy which could successfully challenge the British and which could later be used in peacetime to protect merchant shipping and coastal cities from pirates.

Paine concludes by calling for a declaration of independence — a document that is needed for several reasons. No European power will act as a mediator or furnish aid in the conflict as long as America is still a British subject. Too, as long as the colonies remain subject, they have the appearance of rebels. A declaration sent to European countries would not only promote good will abroad but would also allow America to be recognized and received in the foreign courts.

The added appendix gives Paine the opportunity to reply to the king's speech to Parliament, which he views as "a piece of finished villainy" (I, 40). More importantly, it allows him to recapitulate his principal arguments for a declaration of independence rather than a course of reconciliation. He concludes by expressing the belief that, if America wins independence by the legal voice of the people in Congress, "we have the opportunity and every encouragement before us, to form the noblest, purest constitution on the face of the earth. We have it in our power to begin the world over again" (I, 45).

How are we to account for the enormous popularity of this forty-page anonymous tract? Part of the answer lies in the timing of its appearance. In January 1776 the colonies were ripe for separation. The king had months earlier declared them to be in rebellion, had bargained for Hessian soldiers, and had burned on the very eve of winter the towns of Falmouth (Portland), Maine, and Norfolk, Virginia. Realistically considered, reconciliation was, as Paine termed it, "a fallacious dream" (I, 23). Nor were the colonists resisting passively. Under the command of Washington, the army had regularly engaged the British troops and had even mounted an offensive campaign to take Canada. *Common Sense* simply brought the colonists to the realization that the time for shilly-shallying was done, and it provided the impetus needed to break the last thread in the cord of allegiance which had for so long bound America to Britain.

Part of the pamphlet's success must be attributed, too, to the axiomatic character of the carefully formulated basic principles. As A. W. Peach has observed, "It aimed to review the situation of the colonists in the light of common sense, and the basis of its reasoning rested upon the old human fundamentals of justice and right."[20] We should perhaps emphasize at this point that it was not due to any startling or new insights into political theory that Paine gained the admiration of his readers. On the contrary, his doctrine, based upon the natural-rights philosophy and upon the social contract, was widely accepted as a commonplace in the late eighteenth century.[21] In fact, it would be difficult to trace Paine's political philosophy to its source, for he was influenced by such diverse thinkers as François Quesnay and A.R.J. Turgot, as Baron de Montesquieu and Jean Jacques Rousseau, as Sir Isaac Newton and John Locke. Paine's information came to him, as Professor Adkins says, "from devious and indirect sources"[22] — his wide but undirected reading, the scientific lectures he attended in London, the many conversations and debates in which he had engaged.

The doctrine of natural rights, which lies as the foundation stone upon which Paine constructed virtually his whole philosophical system, was in the very air. It was his heritage as an Englishman; for, it was as Carl Becker has called it, "good old English doctrine newly formulated to meet a present emergency."[23] When Paine outlined in the opening section of *Common Sense* a society of free, equal, and independent men who use their reason to determine good from bad, and who unite into a community and agree to abide by such rules as are necessary to insure safety, liberty, and protection of property, he was but rephrasing the terms of Locke's social compact. When Paine considered the question of how much authority a government so constituted should possess, he simply molded his answer to conform to the kind of government for which Locke had furnished a reasoned foundation: it should possess only enough authority to ensure freedom and security, "for the more simple any thing is, the less liable it is to be disordered, and the easier repaired when disordered" (I, 6). After all, governments exist for men, not men for governments, Paine maintained. Such thinking was the philosophy of the Enlightenment, and, while not new, was seized upon as the sheerest common sense by colonists who chafed under what they regarded as oppressive and unjustified control of their affairs.

While the timing and the doctrine were contributing factors in the success of *Common Sense,* Paine's unique method of address — his rhetoric — was in large measure responsible for the pamphlet's dynamic effect. As Carl Van Doren so concisely asserted,

"Other arguments have been better; none were ever clearer."[24]
Modern rhetorician E. P. J. Corbett has called attention to the fact
that always during periods of violent social upheaval, when the old
order is passing away and the new is coming in, "a loud, clear call
goes up for the services of the man skilled in words."[25] Such a man
was Paine, and such was the call he answered in a manner "hitherto
unknown on this side of the Atlantic."[26] The learned political dissertation, semimetaphysical in theory and Johnsonian in style, was
not for Paine. He wrote politics — propaganda — for the millions,
and his genius lay in his ability to appeal to "the lukewarm, hesitat-
ing and indifferent, and turn them in great numbers to the support
of the cause."[27] He could weave a spell with words, and "no other
man in America, excepting Franklin, was a match for this ill-
taught, heady, and slashing stranger."[28]

Corbett has defined rhetoric as "the practical art by which we
learn how to manipulate all the available means of persuading a
large, heterogeneous, perhaps uneducated audience."[29] Herein lies
the key to the success of *Common Sense:* Paine, realizing that independence could never be won until the colonists united and committed themselves irrevocably, addressed himself directly to this
audience; and he used the rough, idiomatic, commonplace language they understood. And his American audience was a large one
— it was scattered from the rocky slopes of Maine to the hot flat-
lands of Georgia. A heterogeneous lot, the colonists had come
from all parts of Western Europe; most were meagerly educated;
some could barely spell out their letters, others not at all. By and
large, they were small farmers; along the New England coast, many
were fishermen and merchants.

Three of Corbett's "available means" which Paine manipulated
so masterfully to persuade this diverse audience were style, structure, and method of appeal. Over the years, many adjectives have
been used to describe Paine's style. Some have characterized it as
unvarnished, rough, robust; others have noted its lucid, energetic,
and epigrammatic qualities. It is all these and more. Like the back-
woodsman and the farmer for whom it was meant, Paine's style is,
as Peach described it, "homely, always blunt, occasionally humor-
ous, rugged, palpable, overpowering."[30] Above all it is clear, for
clarity is the prerequisite of any good style. The diction is concrete,
with none of the Latinate phraseology of some of Paine's earlier
essays. Always careful to choose words his readers will understand,

Paine avoids foreign words, technical terms, and coinages. The grizzled frontiersman, who would laboriously line out the sentences by the light of his tallow candle, was not to be left in doubt as to the meaning of the words. Therefore, Paine has little use for subtlety and double entendre — all must be plain and forthright.

Paine shows equal care in the selection of image patterns. "The continental belt is too loosely buckled" (I, 44) and "the least fracture now will be like a name engraved with the point of a pin on the tender rind of a young oak" (I, 17) are, for instance, commonplace images that would be familiar but meaningful to the unsophisticated reader. Throughout, Paine evokes images of seeding, reaping, harvesting — activities known to many of his readers. When he told them that "now is the seed-time of continental union, faith and honor" (I, 17), they readily grasped his intent. Also, Paine exhibits a Franklinesque fondness for the epigram. We can almost feel the guiding hand of Poor Richard in such epigrammatic expressions as "'Tis not in numbers but in unity that our strength lies" (I, 31) and "When we are planning for posterity, we ought to remember that virtue is not hereditary" (I, 38).

Paine makes skillful use, too, of other rhetorical devices such as the apostrophe, the exclamation, and the rhetorical question. When he asks, "Why is it that we hesitate?" he logically calls forth a long and reasoned appeal for separation; to pile question on top of question — "Hath your house been burnt? Hath your property been destroyed before your face? Are your wife and children destitute of a bed to lie on, or bread to live on? Have you lost a parent or a child by their hands, and yourself the ruined and wretched survivor?" (I, 22) — can rouse the reader to concur with the scathing denunciation of all Tories as cowards and sycophants. Exclamations like "Dishonorable rank! inglorious connection!" are used to increase the emotional pitch, as is the imploring apostrophe which climaxes the third section of the essay: "Oh! ye that love mankind! Ye that dare oppose not only the tyranny but the tyrant, stand forth!" (I, 30).

With the skill of a virtuoso, Paine modulates the tone of his prose. The following is frequently cited as one of his most eloquent passages: "The sun never shone on a cause of greater worth. 'Tis not the affair of a city, a country, a province, or a kingdom; but of a continent — of at least one eighth part of the habitable globe. 'Tis not the concern of a day, a year, or an age; posterity are virtually involved in the contest, and will be more or less affected even to the end of time, by the proceedings now" (I, 30). In this passage, parallelism, balance, and periodic construction combine to make these lines both sonorous and eloquent. But from the heights of elegance Paine can quickly descend to the depths of invective. He can move with aplomb from denouncing the king as an "ass" and a "wretch" to painting lurid pictures of British butchers wielding bloody swords to the most eloquent call for unity in which each man will "hold out to his neighbor the hearty hand of friendship, and unite in drawing a line, which, like an act of oblivion, shall bury in forgetfulness every former dissention" (I, 46).

As we noted earlier, Paine structures his material in several clearly marked divisions. This careful marking of the various parts of the discourse was again for the benefit of the untutored segment of his audience. We notice, too, that there is a clearly discernible and logical progression in the development. Beginning with the definition of terms, Paine methodically accounts for the origin and rise of government. This preliminary part, elaborated in some detail, serves to give his pronouncements on the British constitution an air of authority which they might otherwise lack. Even within this first part, we can see Paine reducing the arguments at the conclusion of each subject segment.

Having considered the constitution, he logically moves to consider the issues of monarchy and hereditary succession; but not until he reaches the third section, however, does he broach his primary purpose: the call for immediate separation. As he begins to pull out his rhetorical stops, Paine repeatedly juxtaposes calls to action and arguments. From showing the need for separation, he moves to discussing the ability of the colonies to carry it through, which is again a logical progression. "Let us . . . take a general survey of things" (I, 31), he writes; and he proceeds, by means of statistical tables and by closely reasoned analyses of colonial finances, military, and economic conditions to convince his reader that independence is an entirely feasible proposition. The argument comes full circle when Paine in conclusion picks up the line of thought with which he opened the essay. He began the pamphlet by noting that his remarks might not yet be "sufficiently fashionable to procure them general favor" (I, 3), and he closes it by remarking that "These proceedings may at first seem strange and difficult, but like all other steps which we have already passed over, will in a little time become familiar and agreeable" (I, 39).

The method of appeal, the third of the "available means," has a threefold application: the rational, the emotional, the ethical. While Paine described his method of arguing as "nothing more than simple facts, plain arguments, and common sense" (I, 17), the truth of the matter is that his arguments do not fare well when they are subjected to the impartial scrutiny of a scholar trained in logic. Such an expert will disavow the "simple voice of nature" to which Paine appeals for substantiation and accuse him of cleverly leading the unwary reader into the pitfalls of faulty reasoning — which, of course, Paine does. The logician will cite instances of such faults as *ad hominem,* wherein Paine attacks the person of the king rather than the policies of his government; he will point out invalid generalizations, such as Paine's attributing the great distance separating America and Britain as evidence that the one should not have authority over the other; he will label as false deduction Paine's conclusion that monarchy is contrary to the will of God; he will cry false analogy to the comparison between hereditary succession and the doctrine of original sin. While from a technical point of view much of Paine's argumentative method may be found wanting, the important fact is that he nevertheless convinced his reader, who was, after all, even less learned and philosophical than Paine. What did it matter to the frontiersman and the farmer that Paine's reasoning was not irrefutable? It made the greatest "common sense" to him. The arguments, as Tyler says, were "exactly fitted to the hour, to the spot, and to the passions of men."[31]

Not only did Paine intend for his arguments to convince his reader, he also made a deliberate appeal to the reader's emotions in order to make that objective seem desirable. The writer of persuasion always has the problem of deciding which emotional appeals are best likely to succeed with the majority of his readers. Since many of the colonists had large families, Paine decided to appeal to familial devotion. Knowing that parents have strong feelings where their children's safety and well-being are involved, he repeatedly urges the reader to pursue a course of immediate separation in order to spare his child bloodshed in his time. Colonial status is no fit bequest for posterity, he admonishes; and shrinking back now will merely be "leaving the sword to our children" (I, 24). In numerous other ways Paine heightens the emotional appeal:

pejorative terms, such as references to the king's ministers; vivid sensory detail, such as references to burned and looted property, bloody corpses, and ravished women; honorific terms, such as references to the colonials' spirit of good order, their able and experienced men, their virtue and their goodness.

The ethical appeal, as Professor Corbett has indicated, can be the most effective of the three methods of appeal and is absolutely vital in persuasion. In this method, the author's task is to create an impression, through the speech itself, that he is a good man — a man who can be trusted, a man of good sense, good taste, and good judgment. By his words alone, he must convince the reader that his motives are entirely selfless and that his reader's welfare alone prompts him to action.

We can look first at Paine's introduction, for the character of the persona is established at the outset. In order to enlist the good will of the reader, Paine refers admiringly to "the good people of this country" and professes sympathy for their having been so "grievously oppressed." He is quick, however, to belay any suggestion that he blames them for the present ills of the country; he suggests that they have tolerated the oppression for so long they have begun to become accustomed to it. In the introduction, he also disavows any personal motives: he "studiously avoided everything which is personal among ourselves"; he is connected to no party; he is under no sort of influence but that of reason and principle. He is simply a lover of mankind, he continues, and his concern is that of any man "to whom nature hath given the power of feeling" (I, 3.4).

That Paine reads his audience well is shown by the degree of respect he accords to the ideals that they cherish and to the things they reverence. For example, he gives throughout the pamphlet the impression of being a very devout Christian. Actually, Paine was a Deist who would a few years later openly deny the validity of much of the Christian doctrine. Knowing, however, that most of his readers had been reared as Protestants, many of whose forefathers had been leaders of the dissenting sects, he shows a very deep respect for the Bible, a hatred of the devil, distrust of Roman Catholics, and himself to be a God-fearing man. In fact, he rested his case against monarchy almost entirely on scriptural authority. Furthermore, the character he projects is one who subscribes to the Puritan work ethic. Realizing the value that the average colonist placed upon the man who by dint of his own labor provides for his family, he casts aspersion upon the king for not having any work to do. Such idle people only stir up trouble: "A king hath little more to do than make war and give away places" (I, 16).

As the tract unfolds, Paine continues to build the character of the persona. To identify with the colonists, he consistently uses the pronoun "we" and speaks to the reader as "friend." He makes the reader's cause his cause: "a government of our own is our natural right" (I, 29). The persona emerges as a responsible man who will not shirk his duty today to have it fall upon his children's shoulders tomorrow. And, knowing most of the colonists to be simple people, Paine gives the impression that he, too, is a commonplace person. He would have them think him knowledgeable, but not intellectual. When he offers his plan for representative government, for example, he is careful to affirm that "I have no other opinion of them myself, than that they may be the means of giving rise to something better" (I, 27). Such modesty can be seen only as an admirable trait. A fair man who wants to do the right thing, he has no interest in power and wealth by conquest. He desires only to tend to his business of commerce and to live in peace. And it is on this note that Paine closes the pamphlet, for he desires only that all men be good neighbors, good citizens, good friends.

The consummate skill with which a strong ethical appeal is exerted goes far in explaining the unprecedented popularity of *Common Sense.* As an individual, Paine was wholly unknown to the audience, yet through his words he projects a character who is strong and forceful, possessed of sound sense, good moral character, and unquestionable integrity.

From our vantage point of two hundred years, we can identify Paine's propaganda pieces as the most important pamphlet of the Revolution. Like an electric shock, it galvanized the large number of colonists who were deeply resentful of British policy but who, because of tradition and custom, were hesitant to face squarely the issue of separation. As F. J. McConnell has stated, Paine "crystallized the majority discontent and brought it to a crisis."[32] Although Jefferson had written more than two months after Bunker Hill that he was "looking with fondness towards a reconciliation with Great Britain,"[33] the majority of Whigs — and Jefferson with them — had within six months of the publication of *Common Sense* turned completely around and openly declared for the independence which before that time had so vehemently been repudiated.

Paine himself viewed the importance of the pamphlet as such "that if it had not appeared, and that at the exact time it did, the Congress would not now have been sitting where they are. The light which that performance threw upon the subject gave a turn to the politics of America which enabled her to stand her ground" (II, 1163). While many will not assign the pamphlet such an importance as did its author, we should remember that it did make a significant contribution: it prepared the minds of plain men for independence, and it shifted their loyalty from the British crown to the American republic.[34]

### III    The Forester vs. Cato

While *Common Sense* was holding sway among the common people, many in the upper classes, especially the Tories and the conservative Whigs, became alarmed at the widespread acceptance of Paine's outspoken call for independence. It is a measure of the pamphlet's success that printed attacks on it were few, however, and that those were largely ineffectual.[35] The most serious of these efforts was a series of newspaper letters which appeared in the *Pennsylvania Gazette* during April 1776. Signed "Cato," these attacks on *Common Sense* were written by an aristocratic Anglican clergyman, Dr. William Smith, Provost of the College of Philadelphia and an outspoken Tory. A strong advocate of reconciliation, Smith, first, repudiated the republicanism which Paine's pamphlet was fostering among the populace and cautioned against following a dangerous course of independence, and, second, attacked Paine personally by sneering at him for being a foreigner (Smith himself was a Scotsman and his wife was English).

Paine answered "Cato" in a series of four letters which first appeared in the April 3, 10, 24, and the May 8, 1776 numbers of the *Pennsylvania Journal*. Signing his letters "The Forester," Paine defended and expanded the arguments of *Common Sense*. That he did not hesitate in the least to accept this challenge from a learned adversary is indicated by the conclusion of his first letter: "Remember thou hast thrown me the glove, Cato, and either thee or I must tire. I fear not the field of fair debate, but thou hast stepped aside and made it personal. Thou hast tauntingly called on me by name; and if I cease to hunt thee from every land and lurking hold of mischief, and bring thee not a trembling culprit before the public bar,

then brand me with reproach, by naming me in the list of your con-
federates'' (II, 65).

As for being a foreigner, Paine replies ''A freeman, Cato, is a
stranger nowhere — a slave, everywhere'' (II, 69). He scorns Cato's
letters as being ''gorged with absurdity, confusion, contradiction
and the most notorious and wilful falsehoods'' (II, 61); and he
derides his manner of writing: it ''has as much order in it as the
motion of a squirrel. He frequently writes as if he knew not what to
write next, just as the other jumps about, only because it cannot
stand still'' (II, 60). Paine, of course, could hold his own with anyone — and best most of them — in any battle of words. *The
Forester's Letters* were reprinted in numerous other colonial newspapers and served to heighten even further the growing desire for a
declaration of independence.

## IV  *A Series of Crises*

When in July 1776 the Congress formally declared the colonies to
be free and independent states, Paine promptly resigned his editorial position and enlisted in a division of the ''flying camp,'' a
body of militia and volunteer soldiers that was to be sent wherever
needed. When his brief term of service expired, he went to Fort Lee
on the Hudson as aide-de-camp to General Nathanael Greene, with
whom he saw action throughout the late summer and fall.

The campaign of 1776 did not bode well for the Americans. In
fact, up to the very end of the year, it was disastrous. Under the
command of General Washington, the army was routed from Long
Island in August; in September, it was forced to abandon New
York; in October, White Plains was lost; in November, Forts Washington and Lee fell. In all these ''calamitous, and distressing expe-
riences, — defeats, retreats, marchings, and countermarchings,
before a victorious and scornful foe,''[36] Paine seems to have par-
ticipated. Buffeted by snowstorms, the bedraggled army steadily
retreated; and its strength dwindled as the weather and the expiring
enlistment periods took their toll. By the end of November, the
situation was critical. Realizing that somehow the dispirited troops
must be rallied and the citizenry stirred to renewed action, Paine
sharpened his eagle quill pen and, marching by day and writing on
a drumhead by the campfire by night, composed the first number
of *The American Crisis*. Even as he put the finishing touches on his
manuscript, Washington raced for the Delaware River, which he

crossed "even as Cornwallis snapped at his heels."[37] Paine's first
*Crisis* paper went to the printer in the same dispatch bag with
Washington's despairing letter to his kinsman Lund Washington:
"Your imagination can scarce extend to a situation more distressing
than mine," the general wrote. "Our only dependence now is upon
the speedy enlistment of a new army. If this fails, I think the game
will be pretty well up...."[38]

*Crisis* I, which was printed on December 19, 1776, just six days
before Washington's surprise attack on the Hessian troops at Trenton, appealed in ringing phrases to the emotions "that stir the
hearts of men — love of home and country, anxiety, hope, resentment...."[39] While much of the rhetoric of the Revolution has been
forgotten, the opening lines of this first *Crisis* live on: "These are
the times that try men's souls. The summer soldier and the sunshine
patriot will, in this crisis, shrink from the service of their country;
but he that stands it *now,* deserves the love and thanks of man and
woman" (I, 50). As a propagandist, Paine is at his finest hour.
Washington was so moved by Paine's message that he ordered the
pamphlet read aloud to his assembled troops before they went into
battle.

As in *Common Sense,* Paine's expressed purpose in *Crisis* I is to
"bring reason to your ears, and, in language as plain as A, B, C,
hold up truth to your eyes" (I, 56). Of the recent military disasters,
he writes that "...no great deal is lost yet"; and he maintains that
God will "not give up a people to military destruction ... who
have so earnestly and so repeatedly sought to avoid the calamities
of war, by every decent method which wisdom could invent..." (I,
50). He finds the widespread panic beneficial, for it will serve to
expose secret traitors; he praises Washington's firmness of mind
and his fortitude; he denounces the Tories in a slashing attack; he
issues a call for a permanent army for the duration of the war; and
in a passage of sustained eloquence he pleads for help from every
quarter. "Let it be told to the future world," he writes, "that in the
depth of winter, when nothing but hope and virtue could survive,
that the city and the country, alarmed at one common danger, came
forth to meet and to repulse it" (I, 55).

After justifying the taking up of arms as a defensive measure,
Paine outlines the disastrous results of acceding to British demands
for surrender and issues a final call to courage calculated both to
alarm and incense: "By perseverance and fortitude we have the

prospect of a glorious issue; by cowardice and submission, the sad choice of a variety of evils — a ravaged country — a depopulated city — habitations without safety, and slavery without hope — our homes turned into barracks and bawdy-houses for Hessians, and a future race to provide for, whose fathers we shall doubt of'' (I, 57).

Certainly we must ascribe to this vigorous paper some of the credit for the victory which came early in the dawn hours of December 26, when the Continentals surprised the Hessians at Trenton. If we judge it from the standpoints of the needs that it was meant to meet, we must, with George Creel, admit that "literature holds no finer piece of writing than the first 'Crisis'...."[40]

Paine's Trenton musket had hardly cooled, as Conway put it, when his second *Crisis* number appeared on January 13, 1777. In an open letter, Paine addressed Lord Howe; and his purpose was to "expose the folly of your pretended authority as a commissioner; the wickedness of your cause in general; and the impossibility of your conquering us at any rate" (I, 69).

As a friend of Franklin in London and brother of the British commander-in-chief in America, Richard Viscount Howe had come to America as a representative of the ministry and was prepared to offer a full pardon to all colonists who would desist from rebellion and who would lend their aid in restoring peace. Paine berates Howe's proclamation and denies that he has any real authority. With rapierlike thrusts, he turns upon his lordship his own points. As Professor Peach has noted, and with a display of sardonic humor, Paine's plain language in this number is "uncouth and vulgar even in eighteenth-century controversial diction"; but Peach also suggests that the vigorous, even vulgar, terms and phrases were the result of deliberate planning.[41]

Paine again denounces the Tories, charges the British with acts of barbarity, and prophesies the downfall of the Empire. He scoffs at the idea of the British defeating the Americans: If you retained possession of each position as you won it, he tells Howe, "your army would be like a stream of water running to nothing. By the time you extended from New York to Virginia, you would be reduced to a string of drops not capable of hanging together; while we, by retreating from State to State, like a river turning back upon itself, would acquire strength in the same proportion as you lost it, and in the end would be capable of overwhelming you" (I, 68). After pointing out the weaknesses of the British military, Paine restates his strongest argument: "the more surface you spread over, the thinner you will be, and the easier wiped away" (I, 70).

On April 17, 1777, Paine was elected secretary to the Committee for Foreign Affairs of the Congress; and two days later, on the second anniversary of the Battle of Lexington, he published the third *Crisis*. With no ready subject at hand, Paine announces that this number will be "made up rather of variety than novelty, and consist more of things useful than things wonderful" (I, 75). Going back to the Declaratory Acts, he reviews the progress of the conflict, looks over his principal arguments in support of independence, and examines the progress the doctrine has made "among the various classes of men" (I, 84). Paine at this date had apparently abandoned all hope of persuading the Tories to forswear allegiance to the king, for he now regards them as actual traitors. They are "either a set of avaricious miscreants, who would sacrifice the continent to save themselves, or a banditti of hungry traitors, who are hoping for a division of the spoil" (I, 100). And, in order "that the public characters of all men should *now* be fully understood" (I, 99), Paine proposes that every colonist be required to swear an oath of allegiance to the United States and to pay an annual property tax of ten to twenty percent. The citizen taking the oath, however, would not pay the tax but would instead give his service to the country. Those refusing the oath would be taxed, and the collected funds would be used to support the war.

Paine wrote the fourth *Crisis,* the shortest in the series, on September 12, 1777, the day following Washington's defeat at Brandywine Creek. Exhibiting his characteristic confidence, Paine makes light of the British victory by claiming that it has simply weakened even further an already debilitated British force: "What they have gained in ground, they paid so dearly for in numbers, that their victories have in the end amounted to defeats" (I, 102). We may even lose a few more battles, he advises; but then the British, cut off from supplies and growing smaller with every engagement, will be "in a condition to be afterwards totally defeated" (I, 103).

In addition to accounting for the defeat, Paine praises the courage and loyalty of the troops, exhorts them to renewed efforts, and calls upon each citizen to give his full support to the army. "You, sir," he addresses Lord Howe in conclusion, "are only lingering out the period that shall bring with it your defeat.... We fight not to enslave, but to set a country free, and to make room upon the earth for honest men to live in" (I, 104–105). The winter of 1777–78 proved to be, however, one which tested the mettle of the patriot leadership, for morale in the army was at an all-time low. While the British warmed themselves before the fireplaces of an occupied Philadelphia, the Continentals shivered in rude shelters at Valley Forge. The command ranks were torn by dissension, and even Washington himself was under attack. Paine, whose finger was ever on the national pulse, perceived the need for another *Crisis,* and, in the intervals between collecting and presenting intelligence reports to the Pennsylvania Assembly and carrying out his duties as Congressional secretary, he began composition of the fifth number that appeared March 21, 1778, and was dated at Lancaster, Pennsylvania.

Blandly ignoring the exigencies of the moment, Paine exudes enthusiasm in the opening pages of the fifth *Crisis.* "It is pleasant to look back on dangers past," he writes, with the complacence of a sure winner. "The long doubtful winter is changing to sweeter prospects of victory and joy" (I, 111). In the first part of the paper, an address "To General Sir William Howe," Paine exhibits a method that was to become one of his principal weapons in controversy — the combining of ridicule and jest with incisive argument.[42] He taunts Howe by constantly referring to him as "Sir William" (Howe had recently been elevated to the peerage), and he ponders with mock seriousness the type of monument that America should erect to his memory — for "America is anxious to bestow her funeral favors upon you." He finally decides that "In [a] balmage, sir, of humble tar, you will be as secure as Pharaoh, and in a hieroglyphic of feathers, rival in finery all the mummies of Egypt" (I, 108).

Having done with heavy-handed humor, Paine accuses Howe of having "imported a cargo of vices blacker than those which you pretend to possess" (I, 109); and he cites as Howe's most dastardly act the distribution of counterfeit colonial currency. He reviews Howe's three campaigns in America and concludes that they resemble nothing so much as a puppy chasing its tail: "You have moved in and out, backward and forward, round and round, as if valor consisted in a military jig" (I, 114). He chides him for occupying Philadelphia — an act "dictated by fear ... hiding yourself among women and children, and sleeping away the choicest part of the

campaign in expensive inactivity" (I, 116). By singling out General
Howe for his scathing attack, Paine hoped to draw together the
wrangling patriots by reminding them that, after all, they did have
a common enemy and that he was in their midst.

The second part of the paper, addressed to the inhabitants of
America, evinces the same unbounded optimism as the first part.
There is no need to hold up Greece and Rome as objects of excellence and imitation, claims Paine, for "America has surmounted a
greater variety and combination of difficulties, than, I believe, ever
fell to the share of any one people" and has brought about "the
most virtuous and illustrious revolution that ever graced the history
of mankind" (I, 123). Hastily reviewing present affairs, Paine finds
even the loss of Philadelphia to be more advantageous than otherwise. He can see victory within sight, and he exhorts the country to
bend its whole attention to repulsing Howe's army, for "the instant
that the main body . . . is defeated, all the inferior alarms throughout the continent, like so many shadows, will follow his downfall"
(I, 127). And in conclusion he offers to the nation his own plan,
based on a quota system, for recruiting and sustaining an army.

Early in 1778 Parliament offered peace proposals which would
have given the colonies everything they wanted except independence. Confident that the Americans would accept their terms, the
ministry promptly dispatched a five-member commission to negotiate the settlement. When the Congress, however, refused to consider any terms which failed to accord the colonies independence,
the commission issued a Manifesto and Proclamation directly to
the American people, advising them to overthrow the Congress and
accept the offers of peace. It was to the Manifesto and Proclamation that Paine replied in the sixth *Crisis* in the name of the American people on October 20, 1778. Addressing himself to the commissioners, Paine, predictably, regards the Proclamation with con-
tempt. With the specific purpose of lessening any influence it might
be having on the citizenry, he answers certain sections of the
document.

First, he considers the commission's charge that in allying with
France America has mortgaged herself to the enemy. He defends
the treaty as "open, noble, and generous . . . founded on sound
philosophy, and neither a surrender or mortgage. . . ." (I, 132). To
the threat to lay America in waste, he replies that Britain's loss
would be infinitely greater than any she could inflict. Never one to

veil his threats, Paine bluntly warns the commission to come to its senses. Second, he gives an outraged reply to the Proclamation's invitation to the American soldiers to do their fighting under the flag of England. Such a proposition is a "universal affront to the rank which man holds in the creation," Paine charges, and "an indignity to him who placed him there" (I, 135). Third, he heatedly rejects the commission's reference to France as the natural and mutual enemy of both countries: "I deny that she ever was the natural enemy of either; and that there does not exist in nature such a principle" (I, 136). Dusting off his hands, as it were, Paine scoffs at the commission for thinking that Americans "with nearly half your army prisoners, and in alliance with France, are to be begged or threatened into submission by a piece of paper" (I, 137). Almost as an afterthought he notes that now the tables are turned: "There was a time when Britain disdained to answer, or even hear a petition from America. That time is past and she in her turn is petitioning our acceptance" (I, 138).

The seventh *Crisis,* which appeared a month later on November 21, 1778, was addressed to the people of England. Unlike the previous papers in the series, this one is restrained; it is largely free of invective and heavy emotional appeal. As Peach has said, "the reasoning is close, tenacious, and controlled . . . [and] the general character . . . is on a high level of restrained argument."[43] Paine explains to the English that they have been duped by a conniving ministry whose driving aim has been conquest, not conciliation. The army, too, has proven itself to be "low, cruel, indolent and profligate" (I, 143), he tells them, and its behavior alone would justify separation.

What advantages would Britain gain by defeating America? To the people as a whole, there would be none, Paine answers. A tax increase to pay for the war is all they could look for. To Parliament, the division of spoils would bring only contention, for the crown would disallow its claims. To the merchants and manufacturers, there would be no gain, for trade would be ruined. To the ministry, the only benefit would be the knowledge that it had been responsible for bringing about the ruin of the country.

Had the British government set about preparing America for independence at the conclusion of the Seven Years War and worked toward constructing a mutually agreeable alliance, the present trouble would have been avoided, Paine claims. Such a plan was not carried out because "the caterpillar circle of the court had an interest to pursue" (I, 155); its members would have found themselves out of their lucrative court-appointed situations in an independent America. Paine advises the English to "risk a revolution and call a Congress.... America has set you the example, and you may follow it and be free" (I, 155). With the fate of America yet hanging in the balance, Paine is already flashing signals to the English that he is not only willing and able but also anxious to help bring revolution to the land of his birth.

No *Crisis* was written in 1779. Much of Paine's time was taken up during the early months of the year in the Congressional investigation of the Silas Deane controversy, a political scandal of such proportions that Paine's zeal in bringing to public attention the true facts eventually cost him his job. A complicated and as yet unresolved affair, the central issue of the scandal concerned the matter of payment for military supplies which Deane had secured from the French government. In his capacity as Congressional clerk, Paine had access to certain documents which indicated that Deane was guilty of collusion and fraud. When Paine published portions of this information in the newspapers, the pro-Deane faction in Congress accused him of violating his oath; and it was able to bring enough pressure to bear to force Paine's resignation.

Following this debacle, Paine felt the pinch of actual poverty and was finally forced to hire himself out as a clerk in a law office at a common clerk's wages. In desperation, he reminded the Executive Council of Pennsylvania of his services to the Revolution, and in November he received the news that he had been elected Clerk of the Pennsylvania Assembly. Comfortably situated once more, Paine was soon able to begin work on the eighth *Crisis,* which appeared some four months later in March 1780. Addressing himself once again to the people of England, Paine is brief and to the point. Instead of seeking to enlist sympathy for the cause of America, he suggests that England is now "in the condition of an endangered country" (I, 159); for the exploits of Captain John Paul Jones have brought it a real threat of American invasion. Pursuing this theme, he maintains that the other nations of Europe will not lift a finger to help England if she is invaded; indeed, "the natural feelings of every rational being will be against you" (I, 161).

Paine has frequently been called our "first internationalist," and

in the final paragraph of this number we find evidence to corrob-
orate this view. Foreshadowing his later plan for the establishment
of an international organization to promote world peace, Paine
ascribes the Englishman's arrogance and narrowness of mind to the
fact that he is too much like his island-home; for the Englishman is
"bounded by the foggy confines of the water's edge, and all
beyond affords to him matters only for profit or curiosity, not for
friendship." Such an insular, nationalistic outlook needs to be set
aside in favor of the "larger intellectual circuit." In short, the
Englishman needs to be liberated from the prejudice of an island"
(I, 164).

After years of fighting in the middle colonies, the war in 1780
moved south. The breezes which fanned northward in the spring,
however, struck chill in the hearts of the Philadelphia patriots, for
they murmured of defeat in Georgia and siege at Charleston. And
the report from Washington which Paine read to the Pennsylvania
Assembly served only to deepen the pervasive gloom. The troops
were destitute and exhausted, Washington wrote, and "we see in
every line of the army the most serious features of mutiny and sedition."[44] Knowing that Congress lacked funds with which to pay the
army, Paine proposed to raise money by establishing a volunteer
subscription list, and he contributed his entire salary of five hundred dollars to it. So successful was his appeal that the fund of hard
money not only supplied the army but eventually became the basis
of the Bank of North America.

While awaiting news of the fate of Charleston, Paine penned the
ninth *Crisis,* which came out on June 9, 1780. Even in this gloomy
time, Paine maintains that optimism which manages to turn defeat
into victory. If we do lose Charleston, he tells the reader, it will
serve a useful purpose, for the loss will "rouse us from the slumber
of twelve months past, and renew in us the spirit of former
days..." (I, 166–67). The enemy attacked Charleston, Paine
argues, because it was incapable of winning in the Northern or middle colonies; it is merely "a flourish of honor to conceal disgrace"
(I, 167), he sneers. In a short postscript, he tells the reader that
Charleston has indeed fallen; however, he ascribes the defeat of the
colonies to the lack of a sufficient supply of provisions, not to a
superior British force.

In spite of the boost given by the subscription fund, the financial
situation remained unsatisfactory. Congress lacked the power to

enforce tax measures, and, consequently, revenues from the states were uneven — sometimes none were forthcoming. In *The Crisis Extraordinary,* dated October 4, 1780, Paine devotes himself to the unpopular subject of taxation. Realizing that a uniform system of taxation is both necessary and advantageous, he has as his principal design "to form the disposition of the people to the measures which I am fully persuaded it is their interest and duty to adopt" (I, 182). These "measures" included raising the tax rate to thirteen shillings a person, the minimum amount required to maintain the army and to pay for the government. Lest his reader become alarmed, Paine shows him that this amount is three times less than his British cousin pays and that, in times of peace, his taxes would be only one-eighth of what they would be in England. He suggests that the additional revenue could be raised by placing higher duties on imports and by taxing landed property and houses.

While Paine was preparing to go to press with this *Crisis,* the news reached Philadelphia that General Benedict Arnold had been exposed as a traitor. Because of the "magnitude of the treason, and the providence evident in the discovery," Paine adds as a postscript the details of the planned act of treason, "as far as it is at present known" (I, 186).

Early in 1781 Paine sailed for France. Congress had appointed Colonel John Laurens, an aide to Washington, to negotiate a loan with the French government, but young Laurens refused to undertake the mission unless Paine accompanied him. Though Paine had to bear his own expense, he consented to go. So successful were their efforts that, when Paine and Laurens returned late in August, they brought with them $2.5 million in silver and two shiploads of clothing and military stores. Thus aided, the Continentals were able to deliver a crushing defeat to Cornwallis's army at Yorktown in October. Though the king had lost over seven thousand men at Yorktown, he refused to acknowledge defeat. He delivered a bellicose speech before Parliament in November, and Parliament then voted to continue the war. It was in reply to the king's speech that Paine wrote the tenth *Crisis.*

Dated March 5, 1782, this paper is divided into two sections. In the first part, Paine replies to the king's speech, which he asserts is a calculated effort to delude the Commons and the people. Paine's method is to quote from the speech and then to offer his own comments. As might be expected, those comments were unfavorable to the king and his proposals. He concludes this section with a lengthy quotation from Tobias Smollett's *History of England* which recounts the reprisals that followed the defeat of the Stuarts at Culloden. Obviously Paine intended for his reader to conclude that similar atrocities would be perpetrated in America if the British won. To Professor Peach, this use of historical reference was a "false step" on Paine's part; for, though it suited his purpose, it hardly had a logical application to the "much maligned George III."[45]

The second part of the paper is addressed to the people of America, and it attempts to convince them that recent taxes imposed by Congress are necessary, fair, and reasonable. Of interest, too, is Paine's digression to denounce further the unfortunate Silas Deane, whom he characterizes as "a plodding, plotting, cringing mercenary, capable of any disguise that suited his purpose" (I, 198).

"On the Present State of News," the title of the eleventh *Crisis,* which is dated May 22, 1782, calls attention to the fact that "something is the matter in the cabinet and councils of our enemies..." (I, 208). Paine had received information, which had been verified by Washington and by Congressional leader Robert Morris, that England was trying to break the alliance between America and France. To make the American people aware of these developments and to reinforce the bond with France, Paine wrote this *Crisis.* His sources indicate, he says, that England has "made secret offers to France to induce her to give up America," while, at the same time, she has made proposals to Dr. Franklin "to draw off America from France" (I, 210). Paine defends the French-American alliance not only on the grounds of interest but also on those of principle and honor. The alliance has brought America the respect and attention of Europe, he writes; and "character is to us, in our present circumstances, of more importance than interest." He calls upon the reader to "let the world and Britain know that we are neither to be bought nor sold' that our mind is great and fixed..." (I, 215).

In *A Supernumerary Crisis,* a short paper, dated May 31, 1782, Paine addresses Sir Guy Carlton, who had succeeded Sir Henry Clinton at New York following the defeat of Cornwallis; and his subject concerns one of those unfortunate incidents which seem to be an inevitable consequence of war. A Captain Huddy of the Jersey militia had been captured by the British and had been hanged for no justifiable reason. Appalled that "such a brutal out-rage would ever be committed" (I, 219), the Americans demanded that the officer who had ordered the unwarranted execution pay for the act with his life. When the British failed to deliver the officer, the Americans retaliated by choosing from among the British prisoners a Captain Asgill, who was to be executed in place of the officer. Concerned for the reaction which this act of reprisal might have upon the American public, Paine calls on Carleton to spare the life of this innocent man: "You have nothing to do but to give up the murderer, and the matter ends" (I, 219). Whether due to Paine's *Crisis* or to the intercession of Marie Antoinette, the execution was stayed, and Asgill was eventually released.

In the twelfth *Crisis,* dated October 29, 1782, Paine indicates that this paper was suggested by a speech of the British Prime Minister, the Earl of Shelburne, in which his lordship had asserted that the independence of America would be the ruin of England. Anxious that pending peace negotiations be concluded successfully, Paine hammers the point that England is already ruined, for America is already independent. To plead the cause of England and America before Congress, as Shelburne had expressed a desire to do, would, in Paine's opinion, merely be adding "the wretchedness of disgrace to the misery of disappointment" (I, 223). And he advises the Prime Minister that, "as America is gone, the only act of manhood is to *let her go.* Your lordship had no hand in the separation, and you will gain no honor by temporizing politics" (I, 227).

On April 19, 1783, the eighth anniversary of Lexington and Concord, Washington formally announced the cessation of hostilities between the United States and Britain; and, on that same day, Paine issued the thirteenth and final *Crisis.* Harking back to the bleak days of 1776, he announced in his famous opening that "the times that tried men's souls are over — and the greatest and completest revolution the world ever knew, gloriously and happily accomplished" (I, 230). Paine urges Americans to pause and look "back on the scenes we have passed, and learn from experience what is yet to be done" (I, 231). He passes from praise of America's auspicious beginnings to caution the new republic that it is not to forget its national reputation and that it has to exercise great care so that no blot "be suffered to fall on a revolution, which to the end of time must be an honor to the age that accomplished it" (I, 232).

The primary plea that Paine makes in the final paper, however, is for national unity. In *Common Sense,* he had written that America's strength lay in union, not in numbers; and he restates that opinion in more strident tones here. Noting that the division of the country into states is merely one of convenience, Paine calls for a strong "Union of the States" which will take precedence over the sovereign rights of any individual member. He reminds the reader of "that happy union which had been our salvation, and without which we should have been a ruined people" (I, 232); and he argues that only as a strong union will the nation have importance abroad and security at home. A well-regulated union, he concludes, is "the cheapest way of being great ... the most sacred thing in the constitution of America, and that which every man should be most proud and tender of" (I, 234).

In *A Supernumerary Crisis,* an addenda to the series, dated December 9, 1783, Paine addresses the people of America for the final time. Though the peace had been concluded, Britain had imposed restrictions on American trade in the West Indies, a move which Paine saw as calculated to fetter the commerce of America. This act of aggression, he argues, shows the necessity of a strong union of states. This action by Britain is "but a gentle beginning of what America must expect, unless she guards her union with nicer care and stricter honor," Paine warns. "United, she is formidable ... separated, she is a medly of individual nothings, subject to the sport of foreign nations" (I, 238).

For more than seven years Paine labored in the cause of American independence; and, when his work was finished, he expressed an "honest pride" that "nature and providence" had put it in his power to "be of some use to mankind" (I, 235). Admirers of Paine have been lavish in their praise of *The American Crisis,* and even his bitterest enemies concede that the series contributed significantly to the ultimate success of the Revolutionary movement. To M. C. Tyler, the literary historian, "The history of the long war may be read in the blazing light of these mighty pamphlets." While Paine felt that his pamphlets had "added something to the reputation of literature" (I, 235), they stand alone in the literature of controversy; for, as Carl Van Doren has pointed out, the talents of Paine were "essentially those of a partisan."[47]

A tireless propagandist, he mercilessly flayed the enemy with "fierce scorn and bitter accusation";[48] and he whipped with his words those flagging patriots who were nearly at the limits of human endurance. As works of literature, the pamphlets, it is true, may often be faulted. Constantly on the move during the war years, writing hurriedly and in the heat of the moment, Paine did not always pay strict attention to matters of grammar and syntax, the niceties of prose style. He was always less concerned with practices of good usage than with the urgent need to move to decisive action the timid or vacillating reader. But, as Professor Peach says, "the pamphlets are unique as examples of English in action, not in repose, and in content and manner, they merit the verdict: masterly.[49]

## V  *Other Writings*

In *Peace, and the Newfoundland Fisheries,* a series of three letters published in the *Pennsylvania Gazette* in 1779, Paine vigorously opposes the English demand that the United States relinquish her fishing rights to the Newfoundland Banks as a part of proposed peace terms. The fisheries are of the "utmost importance" to America, Paine contends, and, moreover, she has a "natural right" to them. To surrender them would be "a species of treason for which no punishment is too severe" (II, 193). In the third letter, Paine points out that "there are but two natural sources of wealth and strength — the earth and the ocean—, and to lose the right to either is, in our situation, to put up the other to sale." He believed the fishing rights to be of such significance that, without them, "independence would be a bubble" (II, 199).

While Paine had dealt briefly with the subject of the "back lands," or Western territory, in *Common Sense,* he treated the subject thoroughly in the pamphlet *Public Good,* dated November 30, 1780. Like many of the Revolutionary leaders, Paine had regarded the vacant back lands as the common right of all and as a convenient means of liquidating the war debt. "It is only till lately," he writes, "that any pretension of claim has been made to the contrary" (II, 305–306). An impasse had been reached when Maryland refused to ratify the Articles of Confederation until Virginia had agreed to forego her claim to the frontier territory. Paine hoped to break the impasse by examining the entire question in a public pamphlet.

After carefully studying the original patents and royal charters. Paine concluded that Virginia's claim to the lands was un-founded. As proof, he cited the Proclamation of 1763, which had decreed that the Western limits of the province would not extend beyond the heads of the rivers which emptied into the Atlantic. Therefore, Paine argued, none of the lands west of the Allegheny Mountains could be rightfully claimed by Virginia. And, when independence was declared, he continued, these lands devolved to the sovereignty of the United States for the benefit of all. As to how the citizens might benefit, Paine suggested laying off a new state and selling the acreage for hard cash through land offices estab-lished in all the European capitals. Enough money could be raised in this manner, he calculated, to carry on the war for another three years. The advantages would be all to Virginia, he points out: her trade would be increased, the new state would buffer her from the attacks of marauding Indians, and her tax burden would be lightened.

While Aldridge calls *Public Good* "a work of historical scholar-ship based on painstaking research into rare manuscripts and printed sources,"[50] others feel that Paine's concluding call for a Continental convention for the purpose of forming a Continental constitution is the pamphlet's most notable point. One of the ear-liest supporters of a Federalist point of view as opposed to states' rights, Paine perceived that the principal weakness of the Articles of Confederation was in the failure to define sufficiently and to mark out legally the internal control and the dictatorial powers of Congress. Not until a constitution defined and described the authority of Congress, Paine maintained, would the central govern-ment be able to direct the affairs of the nation in an efficient and progressive manner.

For several years Paine toyed with the idea of writing a history of the Revolution, and in gathering materials for this proposed work he perhaps came across the Abbé Raynal's *Revolution d'Amerique,* which had appeared in an English translation in 1781. Being inti-mately acquainted with all the details of the conflict, Paine discov-ered numerous factual errors in the account and disagreed with cer-tain of the philosophical conclusions. In order to defend America from the Abbé's errors — and some think to acquire a European reputation for himself — Paine published in 1782 the *Letter to the Abbé Raynal.* The pamphlet was well received abroad, where it was soon translated into four different French versions and where it was "enthusiastically reviewed."[51]

Space permits only a listing of the principal "errors" which Paine sets out to clarify. First, he rejects the Abbé's assertion that the basic cause of the Revolution was America's refusal to allow Britain to impose certain light taxes. The real cause, according to Paine, was Parliament's contention that it had the right "to bind America in all cases whatsoever." Second, Paine points out factual errors, such as the Abbé's reference to the victory at Trenton as an "accident." Third, he disputes the statement that America did not reject the British peace offers until after the Treaty of Paris had been signed. As Paine tells it, the British knew of the treaty and hurried to complete their proposals before the Americans received the news. Fourth, as to the Abbé's suspicions concerning the French-American alliance, Paine warmly responds that America saw in the treaty "not a temporary good for the present race only, but a continued good to all posterity." And he brushed aside as meaningless the objection that one party is a monarchy and the other a republic.

Although most of the arguments in the *Letter* are familiar ones, the work is significant, according to Darrel Abel, because it shows a definite step forward in the progress of Paine's political thought. "It represents the stage," writes Abel, "where Paine actually ceased to think in nationalistic terms and became a practical internationalist." Abel believes that, as the war drew toward an end, Paine became more and more aware of its international implications and that, when he had occasion to defend the alliance with France, he found practical grounds for extending his "professed universal benevolence in international rather than merely national affairs."[52] That Paine was aware of the advantages of international federation there can be little doubt, for in the *Letter* he cites the benefits — peace, prosperous commercial relations, relief from heavy taxation, freedom of the seas — which would accrue from such a world federation of nations.

Further evidence of Paine's conviction that the strength and the greatness of the nation rested upon unity is provided in *Six New Letters to Rhode Island,* published in the *Providence Gazette* during December 1782 and January and February 1783. These epistles were occasioned by Rhode Island's refusal to ratify a Congressional proposal to impose a five-percent duty on imported goods as a means of meeting the interest on foreign loans. When the Rhode Island Assembly unanimously rejected the proposal, Paine addressed the series of letters to the citizens of the state in an effort to persuade them that the impost was the most convenient way of repaying the money and that Rhode Island should bear an equal share of the common expenses in order to deserve the advantages of federation.[53] As in *Public Good,* Paine here argues for a federal constitution to supplant the inadequate Articles of Confederation and to ensure a stronger union.[54] "It would perhaps be quite as well were [we] to talk less about our independence, and more about our union," he writes. "For if the union be justly supported, our independence is made secure. The former is the mother, the latter the infant at her breast. The nourishment of the one is drawn through the other, and to impoverish the mother is famishing her offspring" (II, 347).

Paine's last pamphlet before leaving America, *Dissertation on Government; the Affairs of the Bank; and Paper Money,* was published in Philadelphia on February 18, 1786. It was written to counteract a move by the Pennsylvania Assembly to repeal the charter of the Bank of North America, which had angered the citizenry when its directors refused to comply with the popular demand that a quantity of paper money be issued to relieve the shortage of specie. Since Paine had seen the bank grow out of his subscription scheme, Paine believed that its services to the country were "of great value in the organization of a sounder economic and political life in America" (II, 368) and he defended it staunchly.[55]

Paine's procedure in the pamphlet is similar to that in *Common Sense.* He begins by making a careful distinction between the sovereign power in a despotic government and in a republic — a point rather far removed from his conclusion — and leads the reader, step by step, through the process and function of representative government; and each step he presents is a tenon carefully shaped to fit into the mortise of the next stage in the argument's total structure. Paine rests his conclusion on the theory that the bank charter constitutes a contract between the commonwealth and certain individuals; the assembly, therefore, merely acting as agent of the commonwealth in negotiating the contract, does not have the authority to cancel it.

Although opponents of the bank attacked Paine as "an unprincipled author, who let his pen out for hire,"[56] there is no evidence that he was bribed by the bank's officers to write the tract. As Professor Adkins has shown, Paine's position on paper money had not changed since the formation of the bank: "he recognized, as did Hamilton, that only by maintaining a gold or silver standard could the new nation as a whole grow and prosper."[57] To many people, Paine's aligning himself with men of wealth must have seemed a desertion of the common man.

CHAPTER 3

# Search for Republican Government
## in France

BECAUSE Paine had given away all the profits from his writing
during the years of war, he found himself in financial straits
when the final peace came in 1783. "I cannot help viewing my
situation as singularly inconvenient," he wrote to a committee of
Congress. "Trade I do not understand. Land I have none, or what
is equal to none. I have exiled myself from one country without
making a home of another; and I cannot help sometimes asking
myself, what am I better off than a refugee, and that of the most
extraordinary kind, a refugee from the country I have obliged and
served, to that which can owe me no good will" (II, 1228). Aware
of his plight, Washington invited Paine to Rocky Hill. "Your presence may remind Congress of your past services to this country,"
he wrote, "and if it is in my power to impress them, command my
best services with freedom...."[1] When Congress failed to act
promptly, Pennsylvania voted Paine a cash compensation of five
hundred pounds, and the Assembly of New York presented him
with a confiscated Loyalist farm of 277 acres near New Rochelle.
Finally, late in 1784, Congress authorized payment of three thousand dollars.

## I  *Interest in Science*

With his financial problems eased, Paine was able to turn his
attention to the study of science, always his favorite pastime. We
find him sending to Franklin details of a smokeless candle and to
Jefferson a proposal for a type of engine powered by sequential
explosions of gunpowder. The project to which Paine devoted most
of his time, however, was his single-arch bridge. He had noticed

that the European method of pier-and-arch construction was not adaptable to the conditions of many American rivers which were often clogged by ice in the winter. A bridge of a single long span, Paine speculated, would leave the river passage clear of encumbering piers. Though Paine did not invent this type of bridge, his conception of an arch made of a number of separate sections was original. "The idea and construction of this arch," he tells us, "is taken from the figure of a spider's circular web, of which it resembles a section..." (II, 1032).

Paine built a model of the bridge and carried it by sled to Franklin's home in Philadelphia in December 1786. Franklin, impressed by the strength and beauty of the structure, advised Paine to submit it to the French Academy of Science. Eager to visit his aged parents in England and anxious for the approval of the French engineers, Paine packed his models and took ship for France in April 1787; and he carried in his pocket Franklin's letter of introduction to Vergennes, the French foreign minister. As he left behind him a new American nation just beginning the arduous process of framing a constitution, Paine little realized that he was not to see the shores of his adopted land for fifteen long years.

While he was in Paris awaiting the report of the Academy, Paine renewed his acquaintance with Lafayette, the young French nobleman who had served with such distinction in the American army. With Jefferson, then American Minister to the Court of Louis XVI, Paine assessed the tense political situation. France and England, enemies of long standing, were once again threatening to go to war. At issue this time was Britain's support of the Dutch Stadtholder and his Prussian allies against the Dutch "Patriot" party with which France was allied.[2] Paine, seeing an opportunity to build a "political bridge" between France and England, wrote to the secretary of Cardinal de Brienne, the French finance minister, and offered his assistance in bringing about an easing of tension between the two rival powers.

## II  Prospects on the Rubicon

When the Academy committee issued its endorsement of the bridge design late in August, Paine departed immediately for England, where he submitted the plan and model to the British Royal Academy. At the same time, he sent to press his latest pamphlet, *Prospects on the Rubicon,* which he hoped would discourage the threatened war and cement friendly relations between England and France. Viewing the Rubicon as a figurative river of war, Paine, in this first entry into English politics, attempts to reconcile misunderstandings between the French and English peoples. He warns the English to consider the cost of a war with France while there is yet time. All that the English people have ever gotten from war, Paine writes, has been "an amazing accumulation of debt, and an unparalleled burden of taxes." "Wars that might have been prevented," he admonishes, "have been madly gone into, and the end has been debt and discontent" (II, 624). Furthermore, he continues, the cause can in no way justify the burdens which will be imposed upon the people. Eloquently, Paine pleads the help of the people: "I defend the cause of the poor, of the manufacturers, of the tradesmen, of the farmers, and of all those on whom the real burden of taxes falls — but above all, I defend the cause of humanity" (II, 632).

France's population is more than double that of Great Britain and Ireland, Paine points out; and, moreover, her revenues are substantially greater. Discussing England's fiscal policy at some length, he cautions the reader not to be deluded by paper riches. Noting that the actual amount of gold and silver in England has not increased in twenty years, he asserts that the nation's wealth has increased only in terms of paper currency and not in terms of real money. Although this economic theory of mercantilism is outmoded today,[3] Paine was firmly convinced that "an increase of paper is not an increase of national money, and the confounding paper and money together, or not attending to that distinction, is a rock that the nation will one day split upon" (II, 638).

Comparing conditions in England and France, Paine warns the English not to be misled by the apparent disorder in France. This is "no more than one of the links in that great chain of circumstances by which nations acquire the summit of their greatness" (II, 634), he writes. Do not think, he continues, that because France appears indisposed to go to war, she is not able to go to war. On the other hand, England's apparent disposition for war, he concludes, is mistaken by her for a condition to undertake and carry one on.

An interesting — and significant — point is that this pamphlet does not possess the antimonarchical tone of *Common Sense* and the *Crisis* papers. There is no denunciation of the king, no strident call for overthrow of the monarchy. As Aldridge has noted, Paine subscribes in this work to the popular theory of the *bon roi,* the idea that the state was a union of the common people and monarch, and the nobles were to be submerged for the glory of the whole.[4] Or, as Audrey Williamson put it, Paine viewed the state as an alliance of the French king and people against the nobility, and he exhorted England to build her own wealth and liberties by uniting the people with the throne.[5]

During the next several years Paine devoted his time to two principal activities: promoting the iron bridge and keeping abreast of events in the active arena of French-English politics. Having secured English patents for the bridge in 1788, Paine contracted with the Walker Ironworks firm to construct under his personal supervision a test span. So successful was the span that Paine had it transported to London, where it was erected on a greensward as a tourist attraction. He was not successful, however, in his efforts to secure the financial backing necessary to undertake the construction of a full-scale bridge. So, as the months wore away and as his high hopes for the bridge faded, Paine began more and more to follow the movement toward revolution in France and to involve himself directly in the efforts of the radicals to reform the English government.

In Paris, Paine engaged in political conversations with Jefferson and the French leaders. To R. R. Fennessy, "these heady discussions in Paris on rights, principles, and origins of government, elated Paine considerably, and sent him back to England with renewed political zeal."[6] So zealous, in fact, was Paine that he proposed to Jefferson that he serve unofficially as American minister to the English court. Congress could utilize his extensive connections, he claimed, and save the expense of replacing John Adams, who was retiring as minister to Great Britain.

### III   *Paine and Burke*

Back in England in the summer of 1788, Paine, now an honorary member of the Society for Constitutional Reform, met the eminent statesman Edmund Burke by means of a letter from his American friend Henry Laurens. Impressed with Paine, Burke invited him to spend a week at his home, and he introduced him to many of his influential Whig friends. As to why Paine cultivated the friendship of the politically conservative Burke and the Whig leaders, Fennessy reasons that Paine saw them as a source of political information and that he was anxious to discover how far they would be willing to support his long-range plans to reform the English system of government on republican principles.

It was inevitable that the friendship of Burke and Paine would be of short duration, however. By temperament and by outlook, the two men had little in common; and Burkean metaphysics was to prove extremely distasteful to the journalist with a scientific turn of mind. Late in 1789, when Paine wrote to Burke several times from Paris, his letters reflected the excitement he felt at being in the midst of the revolutionary foment. Burke was probably alarmed at Paine's prediction that the reformers would stop at nothing short of total reformation both at home and abroad. "At present," Paine writes, "France appears to mind nothing but her own business"; but, he added, "the revolution in France is certainly a forerunner of other Revolutions in Europe."[7] No doubt these letters praising the work of the French radicals hastened the break in the friendship of the two men; if not, they certainly aided in turning Burke's lukewarm disdain for the reformers into an open hostility — an attitude generated, Dishman believes, by Burke's fear that the tumult in France presaged other revolutions in Europe — perhaps in England.[8]

On November 4, 1789, the anniversary of the Revolution of 1688, Dr. Richard Price, a Unitarian minister widely known for his radical views, preached a sermon to the Revolution Society in which he praised the French revolutionaries and expressed hopes that the same wave of reform would soon sweep over England. Burke, long uneasy about the growing English support for the revolution across the Channel, was so thoroughly alarmed by Dr. Price's bold public statements that he decided he must make a stand. Determined to stem the tide of support at home, Burke took the floor of the House of Commons and bitterly denounced the revolution in France; he had his speech printed in order to give it a wider circulation, and he announced plans to issue a more complete "public letter." Fennessy believes that Burke was convinced that events in France were being managed by a group of unscrupulous individuals, "abstract speculators in politics, anti-monarchical democrats by conviction," who wanted only to bring about the ruin of a grand, centuries-old combination of monarchy, nobility, and clergy.[9]

Paine, of course, knew of Burke's intention, and he waited impatiently for the publication of the letter. He had promised his friends that he would answer it, and had, in fact, been planning to write a defense of the revolution when he learned of Burke's proposed work. However, he could not structure his refutation until he had Burke's letter in hand. Eight months passed before the document finally came from the printer, and those certainly must have been long months for Paine. Finally, however, Burke's work appeared on November 1, 1780, cast in the format of a long letter to a young gentleman in France and bearing the title *Reflections on the Revolution in France.*

Eight years older than Paine, Burke had been born and educated in Ireland. He had come to London in 1750 to study law, but lack of family connections, among other things, had forced him to forego a law career. He turned instead to writing and in 1759 brought out the first *Annual Register,* a yearly review of affairs at home and abroad which he helped to write for the next thirty years. Burke was one of the founding members of Dr. Johnson's *Literary Club,* and he soon became known to the leading British literary figures of the day. He began to devote himself to politics in 1765 when he became secretary to the Marquis of Rockingham, one of the Whig leaders. Soon he was made a member of Parliament; and, for the rest of his political career, he served in the Whig party.

When the American colonies began to become restive at what they regarded as the repressive taxation and restraints imposed upon them by the North administration, Burke spoke forcefully in their behalf. In his 1774 speech "On American Taxation," Burke argued for understanding and reconciliation. He conceded that Parliament did possess the power to tax the colonies as a source of revenue, but he argued that it should never exercise that right. Instead, the colonies should be allowed to tax themselves — even to spend the tax money in America as they saw fit. In his famous "Speech on Conciliation with the Colonies" (1775), Burke pleaded eloquently for three hours with his fellow members of the House of Commons to give America the same constitutional rights and privileges within the Empire that had already been accorded to Ireland and Wales. He called attention to the "fierce spirit of liberty" in America: "A love of freedom," he wrote of the American character, "is the predominating feature which marks and distinguishes the whole."[10]

Why, then, did Burke, who had defended the Americans so staunchly, attack the French revolutionists so vehemently? Some claimed he did so because he had held the position of paid lobbyist, or agent, in Parliament for the colony of New York from 1770 until the war occurred and that it was in his best interest to support the cause of his employer. Perhaps, but this aspect is only a part of the answer.

## IV   *Burkean Evolution*

No really great inconsistency exists between Burke's stand on the American and the French revolutions. The radical difference in Burke's stand is to be seen in the different types of revolutions which occurred in America and in France. In America, the real issue was taxation, which involved "free trade"; and, as a loyal Whig, Burke sympathized with the colonial protests over Parliament's attempts to bring to a close a long period of "salutary neglect" during which colonists had been permitted to pay little attention to the Navigation Acts, which had attempted to force the colonies to trade with Great Britain. Only later did the issue evolve into one of "taxation without representation," and even then Burke's very presence on the floor of Parliament pleading the cause of the colonists was evidence that the colonies did have "virtual" if not "actual" representation in Parliament when few Englishmen during this period had actual representation in Parliament, but when every member of Parliament "virtually" represented every member of the British Empire. Considering further his advocacy of America's cause, Burke emphasized that, since the "three thousand miles of ocean" separating America from England made it impossible for the colonists to send delegates to the English Parliament, the colonists were placed in circumstances very different from those of Ireland and Wales. Consequently, he advocated that Parliament recognize the colonial assemblies in America where colonists had actual representation and grant to them the right to tax themselves through their assemblies.

Burke never in any instance denied the "right" of Parliament to tax the colonists; but, because of the above-mentioned "peculiar circumstances," he spoke against it. This action by Burke may have been interpreted by Paine and others as sympathy for revolutionary and republican ideas, but nothing could have been more inconsistent with Burke's intention. He spoke against acts of insolence in America, as he was later to speak, with even greater force, against violence in France. At the same time, he desired to help Englishmen in America secure their rights as Englishmen not only for their own sakes but also for the sake of the Empire. He firmly believed that the British Empire could survive only if it adapted to meet changing circumstances, and he felt that those individuals who determined the policies of the state should regard that state as he did — as a living organism, like a tree or a person — and minister to it according to its needs at that particular time, not according to some program or theory. That America could be allowed the degree of self-government and independence it desired and still remain within the Empire was entirely feasible — indeed, Burke advocated such a plan.[11]

Moreover, Paine's optimistic belief that a revolution in England would do away with the monarchy and establish a republic in its place was an ill-founded hope. Lacking much formal education and being more inclined to immediate action than to pondering the lessons of history, Paine reveals in this respect a faulty knowledge of both English and French history. After the Hundred Years War (1337–1453), the French sovereign had become more and more important; and the Estates-General, the nearest thing to a legislative body in the country, had become less and less important. Most of the fighting had taken place on French soil and the disorganized conditions after the war had prompted the Estates-General to grant the king the right to levy the *taille,* a property tax, making him financially independent.

Between 1614 and the beginning of the French revolution in 1789, the French kings had ruled without summoning the Estates-General. Louis XIV, in order to insure his own absolute power, had cleverly undermined the nobles of his day and rendered them powerless. However, before 1789, Louis XVI, one of the weakest of the French monarchs, had lost the ruling power possessed by former kings and had remained virtually a prisoner, surrounded by his court of idle and powerless nobles. There did not exist in France a time-honored institution — such as the English Parliament — that was capable of absorbing the power that had slipped away from the monarchs. The result in France was a vacuum of power — fertile ground for revolution.

In England, power passed, although sometimes not so smoothly, from monarchs to Parliament. As early as the thirteenth century, the idea of a law above the law of the king developed. It can be seen in the work of the thirteenth-century English jurist Henry de Bracton and in the Magna Carta, which limited the power of the monarchy. In later years, this spirit became known as the Common Law, advocated by members of Parliament as a deterrent to the absolute power of the sovereign. While the power of the French monarch increased and while the power of the Estates-General decreased, just the opposite situation was occurring among their counterparts in England. The Hundred Years War, while directly affecting the French people, was seen in England as a faraway conflict of major interest only to the monarchs, whose military exploits led them, time after time, to request money from Parliament. In return for these financial grants, English monarchs accepted limitations on royal power imposed by Parliament. This exchange was effected time after time throughout the centuries; and, as the king's powers were limited, so did Parliament increase in power. In contrast to the situation in France, the English middle class had representation in the government. In 1789, the country was run by an aristocratic and middle-class coalition, and no power vacuum existed for Paine's radical ideas to fill.

Setting aside all other interests, Paine closeted himself and wrote frantically through December and January. When he finished, he took the work to a London printer and bookseller whose shop had become known as a gathering place for radicals like Thomas Holcroft, Thomas Brand Hollis, and William Godwin; and these outspoken proponents for reform gave Paine encouragement and even helped him ready his work for the printer.

Paine had planned to have part I of *Rights* appear for sale on February 22, 1791, the birthday of George Washington; but the printer, fearful of reprisal by government authorities, refused to proceed with the printing. After nearly a month's delay, Paine engaged another printer to assume the job, and the pamphlet was finally ready for sale in March. As with his earlier writings, Paine declined to accept any of the profits; instead, he arranged for his share to be distributed among the various English constitutional reform societies.

## V  Rights of Man, *Part I*

Paine's short dedication to George Washington, the first of several prefatory pieces, offers to the admired American President "a small treatise in defense of those principles of freedom which your exemplary virtue hath so eminently contributed to establish" (I, 244). The brief "preface to the English Edition," which follows the dedication, explains to the reader that this work is an answer to Burke's attack on the French Revolution. Such an answer is necessary, Paine claims, in order to counteract Burke's "flagrant misrepresentations" and "outrageous abuse on the French Revolution, and the principles of liberty. . ." (I, 245).

The work was immediately translated into French, and Paine's "Preface to the French Edition" stresses the idea that the people in all the countries of Europe should consider the cause of the French people to be their cause, but that "those who rule those countries do not entertain quite the same opinion" (I, 247). Wasting no time on niceties, Paine denounces in harsh terms the English government by calling the king "a feeble and crazy personage" and by denouncing the court as "a treacherous court, a demented court" (I, 247). The people of England, however, applaud the French Revolution, he says; and, when they become more fully aware of the nature of the new French government, their desire to follow the same course will be intensified.

With the customary prefatory material accounted for, Paine moves immediately to his principal task — to refute Burke. Stylistically, Paine was no match for Burke, whose prose, with its flowing rhythm and elegantly turned phrases, its subtle interplay between statement and intent, is among the most polished in the language. Paine's language is among the plainest — or the crudest, many stylists would say. Writing again for the common-man reader, Paine utilizes once more those techniques which had served him so well in the earlier American pieces: the blunt — at times coarse — language; the plainspokenness; the accusations which fall like hammer blows; the repetition — always the repetition; the simple, straightforward structuring; the careful summarizing. We must not forget that *Rights of Man,* like *Common Sense,* has a strong propagandistic basis. For, while it was a refutation of Burke and a defense of the French Revolution, it was also meant to convince the body of Englishmen that the course of revolution it defended was desirable for England — and desirable now.

Although Paine does not number the sections of his argument, we shall, for the purposes of summary and explication, consider the work in chronological fashion and assign subtitles to the clearly discernible sections of part I and part II.

*The Glorious Revolution and Hereditary Succession.* The central issue in the initial section of part I concerns the authority of the Parliament of 1688. In that year Catholic James II was forced to flee the country, and Parliament proclaimed Protestants William and Mary joint sovereigns. That event became known as the Glorious, or Bloodless, Revolution.

In the opening pages of *Reflections,* Burke had attacked Dr. Price, who had asserted in his famous sermon that by virtue of the Glorious Revolution the English king owes his crown to the "choice of his people" and that the people therefore have a right to choose their own governors, to put them out of office in disgrace for misconduct, and to construct a government for themselves. In answering Price, Burke made clear his position about the crown and the commons, a position which Paine attacks repeatedly throughout *Rights of Man.* According to Burke, the king of Great Britain did not owe his crown to the "choice of his people"; instead, he was king by a fixed rule of succession.

Because Price had assumed that the choice of William of Orange as king to replace the Stuart James II in 1688 constituted a doctrine of popular sovereignty from which certain rights could be derived, Burke countered with the argument that the appointment of William had been "a temporary deviation" from the established order of succession to the throne. Although members of Parliament would have preferred to crown only Mary, the elder daughter of James II and the legitimate heir to the throne, they had found it necessary to include William in order to prevent those who would recall James II from plunging the country into a bloody civil war. As Burke saw it, the English people were, in this case, exercising a "privilege" rather than establishing a principle; and the principle of rule by succession remained.[12] Following the death of Mary, William ruled a short time alone, and was then succeeded by Anne, the next heir in the Stuart line. When Anne died in 1714, there were no direct heirs to the throne, and Parliament took this opportunity to choose her successor — for reasons Burke would have termed "necessity" — to prevent any Catholic from succeeding to the throne. Still, the Stuart line was maintained through Sophia of

Hanover, a descendant of James I and Anne's nearest Protestant relative, for her son was chosen to succeed Anne and in 1714 became George I, the first Hanoverian king of England.

The Glorious Revolution itself had been triggered by a fear of Catholicism. The birth of a son to James II's Catholic wife meant that the boy would be trained as a Catholic and would take precedence in the line of succession over the Protestant daughters, Mary and Anne. Therefore, Parliament acted quickly to insure that a Protestant would sit upon the throne of England. When William, at the request of Parliament, arrived in England with an army, James II surrendered the throne peacefully and went into exile in France. Thus, by combining the armed force of the ruler of Orange with the hereditary right of Mary, Parliament executed a peculiar type of popular sovereignty, one in which a king was deposed without destroying the principle of hereditary succession.

Second, answering Dr. Price's assertion of the right to put the people's governors out of office for misconduct, Burke maintained that Price had again misunderstood the intent and effect of the Glorious Revolution. James II was charged with more than misconduct; he had attempted to "subvert the Protestant church and state," that is to say, to return England to Catholic rule and possibly to the kind of oppressive rule Protestants had experienced under "Bloody Mary" during the previous century. "This grave and overruling necessity," according to Burke, led Parliament to declare that James II had, by endeavoring to "subvert the constitution," abdicated the government.

When Burke speaks of the English constitution, he does not refer to any one document but to several documents that had come into existence during many centuries. Through the Magna Carta (1215), the Bill of Rights (1689), and other documents, the English people had imposed upon their kings certain limitations that had preserved individual rights and had prevented absolute rule by any sovereign for any great length of time. As a result, Burke answered Price's third point concerning the right of a people to frame a government for themselves by asserting that the Glorious Revolution had not been for the purpose of forming a new government but "to preserve . . . that *ancient* constitution of government which is our only security for law and liberty."[13] Here Burke conceived the constitution to be a spirit of agreement which existed between the two consenting parties to a social contract — the sovereign and his people.

First, there had existed a social contract between the monarch and his people whereby, according to the seventeenth-century English philosopher Thomas Hobbes, the prince gave the people protection, and they gave him allegiance. Although Hobbes never dreamed of a people's "right" to revolution, he assumed that, when circumstances revealed the sovereign's inability to give the people protection, the rulership then passed naturally to someone who could.

In 1642, England was engaged in a civil war between the forces of Parliament and the forces of King Charles I. The beheading of the king in 1649 by Cromwell's forces and the accession of Cromwell to power was, in the world of experience, an expression of what is implicit in Hobbes's theory: the terms of the original contract were by circumstance transferred to the military leader Oliver Cromwell, who was in a position to give protection to the people. By 1688, Parliament realized that an "after the fact" decision about protection of the people was inadequate and that a better understanding of the rights of the people was needed. Since Catholicism was seen as an outside as well as an inside force that threatened the security of the nation, Parliament had acted to remove the threat. It realized that the protection of the people was not enough for the king's part of the contract; there were rights intended in the spirit of constitution which needed to be stated. Thus, the English Bill of Rights (1689) had come into existence as an additional check on the powers of the sovereign. Later the eighteenth-century English philosopher John Locke was to justify the Glorious Revolution on grounds that the people had the right to rebel if a ruler failed to keep his part of the contract.

Burke failed to see anything resembling the right of a people to frame a new form of government emerging out of the activities of 1688–89. Instead, he viewed the revolution as resulting from James II's failure to keep his part of the contract, something Burke insisted was subversion of the spirit of constitution. Burke conceived of the revolution as having been made to preserve ancient and indisputable liberties "[which are] *an entailed inheritance* [that is, restricted to one certain line] derived to us from our forefathers, and to be transmitted to our posterity."[14] Thus Burke added to the social-contract theory the concepts of a gradually evolving constitution and of the responsibility of the present generation to both future and past generations to preserve the contract. In contrast,

Paine emphasized the immediate consequences of the social-contract theory.

To Paine, each generation should break with the past. Thus he was able to reduce Burke's concept of entailed inheritance to an assumption of divine right to govern, which he, of course, believed no man possessed. Furthermore, he maintains that in making this plea Burke has "shortened his journey to Rome" (I, 253). Paine adds a note of irony to his argument when he describes Rome, the seat of Catholic power, as the destination of his opponent; for Burke has posited his entire argument for hereditary monarchy upon the premise that Parliament in 1688 was trying to prevent James II from delivering England into the hands of Rome.

Endeavoring to discredit Burke, Paine argues from the premise that the Parliament of 1688 could not establish a right by assumption; that is, Parliament was not justified in assuming it had the right to bind and control posterity to the end of time. Whereas Burke argued that the English people do not now possess the right to institute a new form of government, and that, in fact, they had renounced that right forever when they had bound themselves and all their posterity to William and Mary and their successors, Paine states categorically that they do hold this right: "Every age and generation must be as free to act for itself, in all cases, as the ages and generations which preceded it" (I, 251).

Paine's argument is clearly an appeal to the needs of the moment, whereas Burke, on the other hand, appeals to tradition. Still, Burke seems to have maintained that the Glorious Revolution was proof of the viability and practicability of the English system of government. Hereditary monarchy had been preserved by a vigilant Parliament, one always alert to encroachments upon the liberties of the English people. In view of this vigilance, why was it not reasonable to assume that a people might surrender certain rights, such as the right to alter radically the structure of government, as long as the system worked? Paine, of course, did not believe that the English government was meeting the needs of its people; and he hoped that, once the people realized how much more freedom the French system offered, they would rebel. Therefore, he bases his argument not upon English tradition, with which he was either unfamiliar or unconcerned, but upon the freedom of each generation to decide for itself. He has stated his argument in the opening section, and his skillful use of repetition and variation tends to heighten its effectiveness.

*The Monarch.* Having dispensed with the matter of the 1688 Parliament to his satisfaction, Paine next counters Burke's charge that the French people had rebelled with unreasonable hostility against a compassionate and legal ruler. To Paine, Burke was "ignorant of the springs and other principles of the French Revolution" (I, 256) when he accused the people of having revolted against the king. Herein we find Paine's thesis: The French nation did not revolt against Louis XVI; rather, it was against despotic principles of government that the nation revolted.

In this section we see that Burke knew as little about the French Revolution as Paine did about English constitutional history. A compassionate man, Louis XVI was certainly not a despot; and Paine rightly perceives that "the monarch and the monarchy were distinct and separate things, and that it was against the established despotism of the latter, and not against the person or principles of the former, that the revolt commenced, and the Revolution has been carried" (I, 256). To Paine, the revolt was against the hereditary despotism of the established government; for, because despotism had invaded every office and department of the government, no course of redress existed except revolution.

He concludes by stating that in other nations revolutions have been excited by personal hatred, but in this instance it was generated "in the rational contemplation of the rights of man, and distinguishing from the beginning between persons and principles" (I, 258). Louis XVI has been described as a good man but a bad king — in contrast to his progenitor, Louis XIV, of whom the contrary might be said. The people, in general, loved Louis XVI; he was genuinely concerned for their welfare, but he always seemed to be one step behind events as they developed during the revolution. As a result, he completely lost control of the government as the revolution became more and more radical.

*The Storming of the Bastille.* Paine's purpose in this section is two-fold: to ridicule Burke's florid prose and to correct his account of the Paris citizenry's taking of the Bastille, the first significant act of violence against the government during the revolution. His opponent's propensity to lapse occasionally into excessive literary elegance Paine turns to his advantage by accusing Burke of theatrics and of manufacturing facts for the sake of show. He upbraids

Burke for giving the reader, not truth, but "the spouting rant of high toned declamation" (I, 259). Paine refers in particular to the following passage in *Reflections:*

It is now sixteen or seventeen years since I saw the Queen of France, then the dauphiness, at Versailles; and surely never lighted on this orb, which she hardly seemed to touch, a more delightful vision. I saw her just above the horizon, decorating and cheering the elevated sphere she just began to move in, — glittering like the morning-star, full of life, and splendor, and joy ... little did I dream that I should live to see such disasters fallen upon her in a nation of gallant men, in a nation of men of honor and of cavaliers. I thought ten thousand swords must have leaped from their scabbards to avenge even a look that threatened her with insult. — But the age of chivalry is gone. — that of sophisters, economists, and calculators, has succeeded; and the glory of Europe is extinguished forever.[15]

Responding to Burke's lament that the age of chivalry was gone, Paine writes: "In the rhapsody of his imagination he has discovered a world of windmills, and his sorrows are, that there are no Quixotes to attack them" (I, 259). Continuing in his jeering vein, Paine berates Burke for his lack of compassion for the suffering multitudes and declares that Burke laments only the loss of aristocratic pomp. In one of the most famous sentences of the book, Paine states: "He pities the plumage, but forgets the dying bird" (I, 260).

Next, Paine moves to correct Burke's interpretation of the citizens' capture of the Bastille and the summary execution of a number of persons. Paine charges Burke with giving undue attention to the Paris mobs, and he very candidly asks why the Englishman fails to mention the Gordon riots of 1780 in London or other riots in Ireland and on the Continent. Sporadic eruptions of violence were not uncommon during the eighteenth century throughout Western Europe, and police were seldom prepared to handle them effectively. Interestingly enough, both Burke and the French government seem to have misunderstood the character of the French Revolution at its beginning. Even before the acts of violence associated with Bastille Day (July 14, 1789) and the subsequent acts of violence that spread to other cities and to the countryside during the remainder of July and August, the authorities, including the king, interpreted this movement as a *jacquerie,* an aimless revolt, and failed to comprehend that it was a popular rebellion controlled by educated middle-class leaders who genuinely felt that they had not been given their fair share of social recognition during the two hundred years of rule by the Bourbon family in France.

Paine perceived that violence was not the aim of the revolutionaries; rather, it was the consequence of misrule prior to the revolution. The outrages which Burke writes about, he concludes, are "not the effect of the principles of the Revolution, but of the degraded mind that existed before the Revolution, and which the Revolution is calculated to reform" (I, 267).

*March of the Women.* The poor harvest of 1788 had not only produced vagrants who crowded the streets of Paris but also had seriously limited the daily supply of bread in most households. Because of exorbitant prices, women shoppers were often unable to purchase bread, the most important element of the French diet. Moreover, the government seemed unable to solve the financial problems of the city. At Versailles, the National Assembly in August 1789 pushed through legislation which seriously limited the power of the king; and it also wrote one of the most famous documents in all history, the *Declaration of the Rights of Man and of the Citizen*, which was a complete indictment of the old system of rule by "divine right." The reluctance of the king to accept the Assembly's accomplishments led the revolutionary leaders to realize they would need the help of Parisian mobs to prod the king if they were to see their ideas succeed. Louis played into their hands by assembling foreign troops at Versailles under the pretense of ensuring protection against the Paris mobs already in frequent disorder. The enlistment of these foreign troops created resentment among the Paris populace, and the revolutionary leaders were able to use this resentment to their advantage.

What began as a disturbance by a small group of women complaining at a local bakery turned into a mass exodus of malcontent women and in a number of men dressed as women. Streaming out of Paris, they chanted as they marched toward Versailles: "The baker, the baker's wife and the baker's boy" — meaning the king, the queen, and the dauphine, who, if they would come to Paris, could surely supply the people with bread. Lafayette followed with the National Guard of Paris. Many bystanders joined their ranks between Paris and Versailles; and, by the time they reached their destination, they comprised a huge mob held in check only by the presence of Lafayette and the guard. After creating a disturbance in the National Assembly, they congregated before the palace; and their force of numbers eventually persuaded the king to sanction the work of the Assembly and to accompany the mob back to Paris. During the night, before the mob and the royal family left for Paris the next day, there was one incident in which a few persons slipped by the palace guard and were killed after they had frightened the queen into seeking sanctuary in the king's quarters. However, showing extreme bravery, the king had shepherded the royal family onto the palace balcony, where they were all cheered by the mob.

In this section, Paine gives a very detailed account of events that led to the march as well as to the events in Versailles. He attacks Burke for omitting the really important facts and for managing others in such a fashion as to produce a "dramatic performance." He accuses Burke of dwelling on the climactic event — the mob's breaking into the palace — and of giving no attention at all to the provoking incidents preceding such an action. Paine referred to disquietude within the city of Paris because of the assembling of foreign troops, an event which throughout the revolution consistently provoked mob action in Paris.

It suited Burke's purpose to "exhibit consequences without their cause" (I, 268) because, Paine claims, it appears that the king's supporters had encouraged these consequences. They wanted to persuade Louis to flee the country, but the Parisians wanted him to come to Paris. "Not less than three hundred thousand persons arranged themselves in the procession from Versailles to Paris," claimed Paine, "and not an act of molestation was committed during the whole march" (I, 272). Paine, who saw this procession back to Paris as a "good day" for the king and the nation, was not able to foresee that, from this point on, not only the king but also the National Assembly would be subjected to the constant harrassment of the Paris mobs and that the revolution would continue to become more and more violent as demogogic journalists like Jean Paul Marat and orators like Georges Jacques Danton held the populace in their sway. Still, Paine's description of what happened at Versailles is much more accurate than that of Burke, who pictures a palace "swimming in blood, polluted by massacre and strewed with scattered limbs and mutilated carcasses."[16]

*Natural Rights and Civil Rights.* Paine used the occasion of Burke's abuse of the French Assembly's *Declaration of the Rights of Man* to set forth his convictions about man's rights. In his usual methodical fashion, he first takes up natural rights, moves then to civil rights, and concludes with a concise summary. While Burke had recognized that man has rights which derive from the advantages of civil society — a right to the fruits of his labor, to educate his children, to his fair share of all that society can do for him — he denied that man has a natural right to a share of the power, authority, and direction in the management of the state.[17]

Paine first accounts for the origins of natural rights. When one arrives at the origin of man, he states, he also arrives at the origin of his rights, for they come from God and had their point of origin at the creation. Moreover, since God made only sexual distinctions between human beings, "all men are born equal, and with equal natural rights" (I, 274). Moving next to civil rights, Paine declares that the natural rights are the foundation of all man's civil rights. He distinguishes between the two by defining natural rights as "those which appertain to man in right of his existence" (I, 275), and civil rights as "those which appertain to man in right of his being a member of society" (I, 276).

While the natural rights are intellectual rights, or rights of the mind, as well as all rights not injurious to the rights of others, a civil right is one which an individual has preexisting in him but cannot enjoy because he lacks the power to enforce it himself. Of this kind are all those which relate to security and protection. When man enters into a society, Paine says, he retains all his natural rights of an intellectual nature; and he surrenders only those which he as an individual does not have the power to execute: "He therefore deposits his right in the common stock of society, and takes the arm of society, of which he is a part, in preference and in addition to his own" (I, 276).

*Natural and Civil Rights Applied to Government.* Having traced man from a natural individual to a member of society, Paine next applies those principles regarding natural rights and civil rights to governments. First, he reviews the sources from which governments have arisen; and he groups them under three heads: superstition (government of priestcraft); power (government of conquest); common interests of society and common rights of men (government of reason). Passing quickly over the first two subjects, Paine discusses at length the type of government which arises out of the common interests of society. Expanding on Locke's social-contract theory — that government should rest on the consent of the governed — Paine stresses the idea that individuals must enter into a compact with one another in order to produce a government. "This is the only mode in which governments have a right to arise, and the only principle on which they have a right to exist," he writes (I, 278). Burke, he says, fails to make any distinction between governments which arose *out* of the people and those which arose *over* the people.

Pursuing the subject further, Paine finds it necessary to define a constitution, and the "standard signification" which he gives to the word is as follows:

A constitution is not a thing in name only, but in fact. It has not an ideal, but a real existence; and wherever it cannot be produced in a visible form, there is none. A constitution is a thing antecedent to a government, and a government is only the creature of a constitution. The constitution of a country is not the act of its government, but of the people constituting a government.

It is the body of elements, to which you can refer, and quote article by article; and which contains the principles on which the government shall be established, the manner in which it shall be organized, the powers it shall have, the mode of elections, the duration of parliaments, or by what other name such bodies may be called; the powers which the executive part of the government shall have; and, in fine, everything that relates to the complete organization of a civil government, and the principles on which it shall act, and by which it shall be bound (I, 278).

A constitution is to a government what laws are to a court. The court cannot make the laws, and it is powerless to alter them, for "it only acts in conformity to the laws made; and the government is in like manner governed by the constitution" (I, 279). While it is true that the English government arose, as Paine said, out of conquest, it also arose and survived because of a social contract, as Thomas Hobbes so clearly delineated in *Leviathan* as early as 1651. Paine did not understand Hobbes's concept of the social contract, based as it was upon a myth that somewhere in the foggy past the people had entered into an agreement with one of their own whom they designated as ruler. As Paine points out, a study of English history does not reveal evidence that any such Hobbesian experience ever happened; and, receiving no support from Locke, Paine was led to declare that England has never had a constitution, and that, try as Burke will, he cannot prove it.

*Advantages of the French Constitution.* Paine was greatly influenced by Rousseau, who advocated a return to nature in order to discover the true laws regarding government; and Rousseau had popularized the idea of the "noble savage" who was noble because he of all men was the least corrupted by civilization. In a similar idealistic vein, he announced that rule should be by the "general will" of the people, that is, the people would act in a responsible manner if they were in harmony with nature. So the power to rule really came from "the people," and governors were in actuality representatives of the people.

With Rousseau's ideas in the background of his thinking, Paine proceeds to indicate the advantages of the French Constitution; and his purpose is to show that it provides for a system of government that is superior in every way to the English system. First, he says, it provides for representation proportionate to the number of electors in any given area (an elector was any citizen who paid a tax of sixty sous annually). He contrasts this representation to situations in England, where a large town like Manchester had no representation in Parliament, while certain very small towns, like Old Sarum, for example, sent two members to the House. Paine is here echoing the strident calls of the English reformers for abolition of the rotten-borough system, a corruption of the concept of "virtual representation" which was not eliminated in England until the Reform Bill of 1832.

Other provisions of the French Constitution which Paine mentions include biannual elections to the National Assembly and freedom to trade, work, and live where a citizen pleases. Game laws and monopolies of any kind are proscribed. Members of the National Assembly may neither hold government offices nor receive pensions; and the king and his ministers, who often act from motives of pride or taxation, no longer have the power to declare war. The right of war and peace is in the nation, "and where else should it reside," queries Paine, "but in those who are to pay the expense?" (I, 283).

Finally — and Paine saves this last item as a leader into his next topic — the French Constitution abolishes titles, which are but nicknames, scoffs Paine, "and every nickname is a title. The thing is perfectly harmless in itself, but it marks a sort of foppery in the human character which degrades it. It renders man diminutive in things which are great, and the counterfeit in things which are little.

It talks about its fine blue *riband* like a girl, and shows its new *garter* like a child" (I, 286).

*The Aristocracy.* For the egalitarian Paine, it is but a small step from denouncing titles to calling for an end to the aristocracy itself. Terming his investigation an inquiry "into the nature and character of aristocracy," Paine first accounts for the origin of aristocracy. It "arose out of those governments founded upon conquest," and it began as a military order "to keep up a succession of this order for the purpose for which it was established, all the younger branches of those families were disinherited, and the law of *primogeniture-ship* was set up" (I, 288). Paine thus begins a violent attack on one aspect of the English system which he and his fellow reformers found especially distasteful: the law of primogeniture. By this law the eldest child, usually the son, inherited the total estate of his parent. "It is a law against every law of nature," Paine writes, "and nature herself calls for its destruction" (I, 288). It results in the disowned children of aristocrats being cast upon the public, he continues, and "unnecessary offices and places in governments and courts are created at the expense of the public, to maintain them" (I, 288).

The French Constitution, Paine declares, has wisely abolished the law of primogeniture; and, furthermore, it does not provide for a body of hereditary legislators, like the British House of Lords. According to Paine, the French decided against having such a house for the following reasons: (a) "aristocracy is kept up by family tyranny and injustice"; (b) the law of primogeniture corrupts any sense of justice or honor an aristocrat might have; (c) the idea of hereditary legislators is inconsistent and absurd; (d) it perpetuates "the uncivilized principles of the governments founded in conquest"; and (e), since these persons seldom marry outside their class, the system tends to degenerate the species.

Paine's statement that aristocracy "arose out of the governments founded upon conquest" (I, 288) again reveals his misunderstanding of the functions of medieval institutions. It would have been more accurate for Paine to have said that the nation-state in both France and England arose from the aristocracy. Out of feudalism came a noble class characterized by individuals who owned property, and this feudal class became the aristocracy and produced the kings of Europe. When Paine declares that the law of primogeniture "is a law against every law of nature," he is clearly thinking of Rousseau's concept of the social contract and not of Hobbes. Primogeniture was a most natural way of preserving feudal society by making it possible for the entire manor — the self-sufficient domain of the feudal lord — to be kept intact. If the manor had been broken up at the time of the lord's death, the economic system of manorialism would have been destroyed, and the serfs would have suffered as well as the feudal class. Whereas Burke would have understood and appreciated the historical role performed by the aristocracy, Paine would have been uninterested even if he had known about it, for his philosophy arose from a different mythical basis than Hobbes's; it was based on the myth that "all men are created equal," and the French Revolution, which Paine applauded, was moving with the new myth toward a clear break with the past.

*The Established Church.* Turning from the issue of aristocracy, Paine then counters Burke's argument for an established church. Whereas Burke had maintained that a state religious establishment was necessary to a free citizenry because it gave them the idea that they ought to act in trust and that they are held to account for their conduct, Paine attacks a state-church connection on the grounds that it gives rise to religious persecution, and he praises the decision of the National Assembly to reform the clergy in France. "Persecution . . . is always the strongly marked feature of all religions," he claims. "Take away the law-establishment, and every religion re-assumes its original benignity" (I, 293). The French Constitution, declares Paine, has abolished both toleration and intolerance because both are acts of despotism. Governments should neither tolerate religion nor practice intolerance of religions. In his natural state man, has "right of conscience" (I, 291).

*The National Assembly.* With a few final observations "on the organization of the formal parts of the French and English governments," Paine prepares to close his comparison. While the Englishman's "rights" are simple grants from the crown, Paine says, the French Constitution distinguishes between the king and the sovereign: it considers the station of a king as official, and it places sovereignty in the nation. The representatives of the nation (National Assembly) are the legislative power that originates in and from the people by election. Thereby, he summarizes, the nation is always named before the king; and the legislative is put before the executive — the law before the king — who is a representative of the nation.

Paine recounts the various designs employed by members of the first and second estates to subvert the National Assembly's work, and he concludes his account of the history of the revolution with the king's ministers fleeing the country, the taking of the Bastille, and the National Assembly's publication of a *Declaration of the Rights of Man,* which was to become the basis of a new constitution for France.

*Summary.* The final portions of part I attempt to "trace out the growth of the French Revolution and mark the circumstances that have contributed to produce it" (I, 298). This discussion is necessary, states Paine, since Burke did not understand the revolution and gave no account of its commencement or its progress. In explanation, Paine speaks first of a "national lethargy" during the reign of Louis XV, in which the writings of the French philosophers showed the only spirit of liberty. In time, the combined weight of the writings of Voltaire, Quesnay, Turgot, and Montesquieu produced "a spirit of political inquiry" which "began to diffuse itself through the nation at the time the dispute between England and the then colonies of America broke out" (I, 299).

When the American Revolution ended, Paine continues, the French officers and soldiers who had gone to America returned and brought with them "a vast reinforcement to the cause of liberty" (I, 300). With knowledge of how to put theory into practice, all that was wanting to give it a real existence was opportunity; and that circumstance was found in the corrupt fiscal policy of the French government. This, according to Paine, was the circumstance which the nation laid hold of that brought forward a revolution.

Paine describes the king's calling an Assembly of Noblemen, the Parlement of Paris's refusing to approve the taxes, and the convening of the Estates-General. He recalls how the third estate, failing to gain truly equal representation, declared itself to be the National Assembly. The king had insisted that the estates vote by order, meaning that the third estate would always be outvoted by the two privileged estates. However, when a National Assembly was declared, he capitulated and instructed the clergy and the nobles to unite with the third estate. Paine briefly summarizes the events from this point on through the composition of the *Declaration of the Rights of Man.*

Drawing toward a close, Paine includes a copy of the Assembly's *Declaration* and a brief section of observations that praises the document as being more valuable to the world "than all the laws and statutes that have yet been promulgated" (I, 316). A short "Miscellaneous Chapter" and "Conclusion" bring part I to an end, but the "Miscellaneous Chapter" continues the attack on hereditary succession and briefly analyzes the British government's fiscal policy. Paine denounces those parasites on the nation who attach themselves to the monarchy for their livelihood. "A band of interested men such as placemen, pensioners, lords of the bed-chamber, lords of the kitchen, lords of the necessary-house, and the Lord knows what besides, can find as many reasons for monarchy as their salaries, paid at the expense of the country, amount to . . ." (I, 326–27). He warns the reader that the present line of kings, having originated with a German elector, have necessarily divided interest and regard England merely as a "town-residence, and the electorate as the estate" (I, 327).

Having done battle with the monarchy and the fiscal policy, Paine prepares to retire from the field — but not before firing a parting shot at Burke himself. "He writes neither in the character of a Frenchman nor an Englishman," says Paine, "but in the fawning character of that creature known in all countries, and a friend to none, a *courtier*" (I, 337–38).

The short "Conclusion" outlines two prevailing modes of government: that by election and representation, based on reason; and that by hereditary succession, based on ignorance. The French and American Revolutions, Paine contends, indicate that "the opinion of the world is changed with respect to systems of government" and that it is now evident that "a general revolution in the principle and construction of governments is necessary" (I, 340–41).

If he is to remain true to his propagandist's creed, Paine cannot lay his pen aside until he impresses upon his reader one final time his principal point of argument; he does so in a lucid yet concise summary paragraph about the role of government which answers his own rhetorical question:

What is government more than the management of the affairs of a nation? It is not, and from its nature cannot be, the property of any particular man or family, but of the whole community, at whose expense it is supported; and though by force of contrivance it has been usurped into an inheritance, the usurpation cannot alter the right of things. Sovereignty, as a matter of right, appertains to the nation only, and not to any individual; and a nation has at all times an inherent indefeasible right to abolish any form of government it finds inconvenient, and establish such as accords with its interest, disposition, and happiness. The romantic and barbarous distinction of (making) men into kings and subjects, though it may suit the condition of courtiers, cannot that of citizens, and is exploded by the principle upon which governments are now founded. Every citizen is a member of the sovereignty, and, as such, can acknowledge no personal subjection; and his obedience can be only to the laws (I, 341).

## VI   *Reaction to Part I*

From the beginning, Paine's book was a sensation. The initial printing of ten thousand copies was quickly sold, and the harried printer ran his presses almost without stopping in order to meet the public's demand for the work. Samuel Edwards, one of Paine's most recent biographers, estimates that at least two million copies were sold in the three months following publication.[18] Made available in cheap editions to almost every reader in England and Ireland, *Rights of Man* was everywhere the subject of conversation. Hardly a newspaper appeared in London that did not have some mention of Paine in it — though, to be truthful, the mentions were mostly unfavorable, since the paper reflected the establishment opinion.

In spite of the negative responses, Paine was convinced that his ideas were taking hold and that the New England he envisioned in print was well on its way toward becoming a reality. In fact, he wrote to John Hall in Philadelphia that "I have so far got the ear of John Bull that he will read what I write — which is more than ever was done before to the same extent. *Rights of Man* has had the greatest run of anything ever published in this country, at least of late years — almost sixteen thousand has gone off — and in Ireland above forty thousand — besides the above numbers one thousand printed cheap are now gone to Scotland by desire of some of the (friends) there" (II, 1322).

While the discontented working class and the ever-present minority of radicals cheered Paine, the government, though aware of his activities, made no overt attempt to silence him. Paine may have felt secure in his position because he claimed American citizenship; at any rate, he continued to make speeches and to pen addresses and newspaper letters "intentionally goading the king, Parliament, and all who believed in the British system of government."[19] His friends, however, began to sense that he was treading on dangerous ground, for it was unrealistic to think that the government would continue to ignore Paine, who showed no inclination to cease his attacks on the monarchy.

## VII   Rights of Man, *Part II*

Being more inclined toward Rousseau's concept of the social contract and his advocacy of republican ideas than toward the concepts of Locke, Voltaire, and Montesquieu, all of whom advocated reform but stopped short of advocating the dissolution of the monarchy, Paine in 1791, while working on the second part of *Rights,* saw in France the possible actualization of his philosophy of government.

During 1791 the French National Assembly completed work on the constitution begun in 1789. Although the majority of the French people approved of the established constitutional monarchy, many leaders wanted to see the revolution run its course and the government evolve into a republic. Inspired by the success of the American Revolution and encouraged by the French progress toward republicanism, Paine envisioned a world revolution whereby all the nations of Europe would follow America's lead and establish true representative governments.

But Paine misunderstood both Rousseau and the American Revolution. Rousseau had talked about a "Republic of Virtue" where men — who were basically good unless corrupted by civilization — served the state not because they hoped for personal gain but because they were virtuous. Although sympathetic to these idealistic ideas, Rousseau still believed that such democracy would work well only in small groups. Paine seems to have been unaware of such limitations, and, incidentally, so were Jacobin leaders in France. They tried to force this idea of republic upon the people, and they eventually produced a Reign of Terror in which thousands lost their heads to Madame Guillotine. Lafayette, to whom Paine dedicated part II of *Rights,* forsook Jacobin ranks and remained moderately conservative throughout the revolution. That Paine continued to think highly of Lafayette even after the Frenchman lost his early popularity among the masses is perhaps a case in point. This regard may have arisen from a sense of sincere appreciation of Lafayette's conservatism, but more likely it arose because Paine always saw Lafayette as a hero of the American Revolution.

But, again, Paine seems to have failed to appreciate the character of the American Revolution. Englishmen in America rebelled against George III in true Lockean fashion because they felt he had not kept his part of the contract. Once independence was established, the three thousand miles separating them from England, plus the fact that George III remained on the English throne, created a Burkean "necessity" for a new government. A republic emerged, for otherwise the Americans would have needed to choose a king out of thin air. Paine seems to have been aware that this extraordinary set of circumstances existed nowhere in Europe, but he felt that the added impetus of the French Revolution made Europe ripe for republicanism.

Paine worked in France until July 1791, and then returned to England to complete the second part of *Rights of Man,* which he thought would complete the campaign to bring the English government to the actual point of overthrowing the monarchy and of establishing a new government based on republican principles. He had hoped to have part II appear on the opening day of Parliament; but the authorities, aware of his plans, pressured the printer into giving up the job. Paine soon found another publisher, however, and the work appeared for sale in February, exactly one year after the publication of part I.

The customary prefatory material of part II consists of a dedication to Lafayette; a preface, which acts as a transition between parts I and II; and an introduction. Burke's statement that Paine's writing deserved no refutation other than criminal justice provided Paine with one of his best retorts: "Pardoning the pun, it must be *criminal* justice indeed that should condemn a work as a substitute for not being able to refute it." The condemnation of Paine's works in the courts would "pass upon the criminality of the process and not upon the work," and, Paine said, "In this case, I had rather be the author, than be either the judge, or the jury, that should condemn it" (II, 350). Paine was far ahead of his time in the thesis he posits for the preface: a government is unjustified in prosecuting a person who merely investigates the principles of that government or its constitution. "The defects of every government and constitution," he said, "both as to principle and form must, on a parity of reasoning, be as open to discussion as the defects of a law, and it is a duty which every man owes to society to point them out" (II, 351).

Eventually Paine was indicted, tried by a packed London jury, and found guilty, in absentia, of seditious libel. The authorities had moved when it became evident that part II would enjoy even wider circulation than part I. Available in a cheap edition, it was readily accessible to the poorer classes — to the very people the government feared would start a revolution. Moreover, Paine made it clear in the second part that he favored the overthrow of the English government; and he was naïve indeed in thinking that the English government would permit this bold advocacy under the guise of, to use his term, "an investigation." Paine was doing far more than investigating the principles of the English constitution; he was declaring that no constitution and, therefore, no legal government existed. There were treasonous implications in what he was saying, but whether his saying it was treasonous is another question. His defender Thomas Erskine pronounced the "futility of any attempt by government to impose on a nation the commandment, Thou Shalt Not Read,"[20] when he charged that the English government by judging Paine had given him grounds for a charge of corruption against the state.

Paine's experience may have had an influence in prompting legislation to insure the freedom of the press, but it would not be accurate to describe him as a forerunner in the modern passive resistance movement, for, unlike Thoreau, he did not advocate breaking unjust laws. "It is better to obey a bad law," he says, "making use at the same time of every argument to show its errors and procure its repeal, than forcibly to violate it" (I, 351). It is the right of the nation, he continues, to determine the form of government, and "the operation of government is restricted to the making and the administering of laws" (I, 351).

The short introduction focuses on the subject of revolution. So tyrannous were the old governments of the world, writes Paine, that nowhere in the old world was man free. "Reason was considered as rebellion; and the slavery of fear had made men afraid to think" (I, 354). "America was the only spot in the political world, where the principles of universal reformation could begin," he writes, and now that revolution has begun in America, the nations of Europe will surely follow. In fact, revolutions may be considered "as the order of the day" (I, 355). "Reason, like time, will make its own way, and prejudice will fall in combat with interest. If universal peace, civilization, and commerce, are ever to be the happy lot of man, it cannot be accomplished but by a revolution in the system of governments" (I, 355).

With this statement in the introduction, Paine makes clear his intention. While part I of *Rights* had attacked the British government, the work as a whole purported to defend the French Revolution. But the intent of part II was clear: the work was written expressly to hasten the overthrow of the British monarchy. No covering matter obscures the essential message, which was calculated, as Paine would put it, to give men — especially Englishmen — the courage to throw off the chains of monarchical slavery.

*On Society and Civilization.* In this short opening chapter, Paine asserts that the basis for order is not government but society and civilization. The foundation of all human order is "the mutual dependence and reciprocal interest which man has upon man." The next step upward, according to Paine, is the mutual dependence that all "parts of a civilized community [have] upon each other." These factors "create that great chain of connection which holds it (society and civilization) together" (I, 357). Government, or much of what is called government, is imposed upon the superstructure of society and civilization. Thus, Paine reasons, government can be done away with and order will still prevail.

Again, Paine's basic concepts are very closely related to those of Rousseau in *The Social Contract:* "In a state of nature ... the strength of each individual is insufficient to defend him ... [so] men merely unite ... and act in concert."[21] Paine is much closer to the English concept of Common Law, however, when he asserts that common interest forms laws and those laws are superior to the laws of government.

As early as the reign of Charles I, English laws, which evolved over a period of centuries by precedence out of the common courts, were considered the Common Law and superior to edicts of the king. Professional lawyers, champions of the Common Law, emerged in Parliament to challenge the despotism of Charles I in the days prior to the English Civil War of the mid–seventeenth century. Possibly Paine would have had much in common with these Englishmen, but not with Burke, whom he dubs "a metaphysical man" because he interpreted government as with but not as a part of natural (physical) law. Burke insisted that government requires experience, "even more experience than any person can gain in his whole life."

To Paine, on the other hand, government was an extension of society and civilization. He asserts that Burke would never understand how the Americans ruled themselves shortly after the commencement of the Revolution, a time when there was no established government. In Paine's view, they merely reverted to the rule of society and civilization, and the experience "led to a discovery of the principles, and laid open the imposition, of governments" (I, 360).

In summary, Paine claims that "government is nothing more than a *national association acting on the principles of society*" (I, 361). It is society, not government, he argues, which is responsible for the harmony that is existent among the greater part of the human family. Man is so constituted that society is necessary for life; in fact, it is essential to his happiness (I, 357). Government, on the other hand, is needed only to supply the few wants which society and civilization are not competent enough to furnish. It is not to government but to "the great and fundamental principles of society and civilization ... that the safety and prosperity of the individual and of the whole depends" (I, 358). The more perfect civilization is, the less occasion it has for governments, which, far from being the cause of order, are often the destruction of it.

*On the Old and New Systems of Government.* In order to prove that the new system of government — that is, one founded upon republican principles — is superior to the present system of kings and court, Paine very briefly accounts for the origin of the present old governments of Europe. The history of the old governments, he claims, can in every case be traced back to groups of armed bandits who overran a country and conquered it. In time, the chief of the bandits — William the Conqueror, in the case of England — "conceived to lose the name of robber in that of monarch; hence the origin of monarchy and kings" (I, 361). Such governments, concludes Paine, can but result in continual war and extortion, for "war is the faro-table of governments, and nations the dupes of the game" (I, 362).

While Paine shows an awareness of English history at least as far back as the Norman Invasion of 1066 and while he emphasizes that the successors of William the Conqueror have "assumed new appearances," he revealed little knowledge of the medieval concept of honor. After the fall of Rome around A.D. 500, no central imperial power existed to control or unite all of Europe; and the Holy Roman Empire never really ruled all of Europe as imperial Rome had done. What emerged to take the place of imperial interest was dynastic interest; that is, allegiance to and struggle between the major families of Europe. Though perhaps completely foreign to the thinking of Paine, we might term the rise of dynastic interest during the Middle Ages as a "grass roots movement" because it began on the local manor where serfs who had no land gave allegiance to members of the feudal class who, in turn, offered not only land but protection from enemies.

This feudal class that owned horses and armor did most of the fighting that Paine refers to, but to label this group as "robbers" is to ignore feudal honor — the metaphysic which held society together during those days. Each feudal lord felt it was the duty of his class to live by a higher code than that expected of serfs in order that law and order might be maintained. Since there was no higher, or imperial, power to which the feudal class could appeal, it was generally agreed that there would be no law at all without feudalism. Furthermore, the feudal class was dutybound to uphold the feudal code of behavior, one that included Burke's beloved "Chivalry."

Since nearly everyone in Western Europe during the Middle Ages was Christian by virtue of being born in Christendom (the geographical area under the direct influence of the Pope), the feudal class, who held the power, felt its duty was to preserve Christian principles. One secular expression of these principles was chivalry, an institution which might be described as the attitude of the gallant knight on horseback who fought for his honor, his lord, and his ladyfair, and who expressed loyalty, kindness to the weak, and generosity to enemies. If this principle "should ever be totally extinguished," says Burke, "the loss I fear will be great," for "it was this opinion which mitigated kings into companions and raised private men to fellows with kings."[22] Whereas Burke laments the demise of "honor," Paine calls for a new day and for an end to the wars that had wracked Europe since medieval times.

Renewing the attack which Paine had first mounted in part I, he turns again to the issue of hereditary succession. It is, first, an imposition on mankind; for this type of government, since man does not have the authority to abrogate the rights of those who come after him, is by nature tyrannous. Second, such succession is inadequate to the purposes for which government is necessary. Paine terms it a system of mental levelling, wherein "vice and virtue, ignorance and wisdom ... is put on the same level" (I, 365). Moreover, the hereditary system is responsible for nearly all the civil wars of Europe, as well as for the foreign wars. Paine concludes his attack with a figure of speech suited to his regard for the subject. "A government calling itself free," he says, "with an hereditary office, is like a thorn in the flesh, that produces a fermentation which endeavors to discharge it" (I, 367).

Turning to the republican system, Paine begins his examination of its virtues with the statement that "it takes society and civilization for its basis; nature, reason, and experience for its guide" (I, 367). Nature, he claims, disperses wisdom indiscriminately among her human children; and the order of government must necessarily follow this natural order or it will degenerate into ignorance. Thus Paine affords himself another opportunity to lash his old whippingboy, hereditary succession. The representative government, on the other hand, takes wisdom where it finds it and is thus enabled to produce wise laws.

At the time Paine was writing this chapter in 1791, real power in France resided in the new Assembly; for the king, who had attempted to flee the country in June only to be caught at Varennes and returned to Paris, had been placed under suspension by the Assembly. With the king under house arrest from June until September, France experienced a limited monarchy in an exaggerated sense. While it is true that there were Jacobin members of the new legislative Assembly who wanted France to become a republic, Paine's open arguments for the supremacy of republican government over hereditary monarchy were ahead of the vast majority of Frenchmen. Members of the Assembly obviously favored representative government since they themselves represented people in certain geographical areas, but they did not necessarily favor a government truly representative of all people. The conditions of the constitution of 1791, for example, limited the franchise to property owners who paid taxes. In September, the king accepted the Constitution of 1791; and, when the Assembly then lifted the suspension, Louis was a monarch truly limited by a written constitution. Most Frenchmen wished the government to remain that way, including Abbé Sieyés, to whom Paine addressed this chapter.

Although Paine failed to question Sieyés's support of the monarchy, we wonder why Sieyés, whose pamphlet *What is the Third Estate?* had been instrumental in the third estate's taking over the Assembly in 1789 and who as late as 1791 admitted that "in good theory, an hereditary transmission of any power of office ... [is] an outrage upon society" (I, 365), was reluctant to end the monarchy? Why was he unable to see elective monarchy as the only alternative to hereditary monarchy? Possibly he felt so because the French people were almost — but not quite — ready to conceive of the nation as an abstraction, an idea, something that existed apart from monarchy. This idea was not to blossom until 1792 when France found herself at war with half of Europe in her efforts to spread the principles of the Revolution — the principles of Liberty, Equality, Fraternity.

This sense of nationalism came much earlier in England and took a different form. There, as early as the time of Queen Elizabeth (1588–1603), perhaps as a result of the threat of the Spanish Armada, the people of this small island began to think of themselves as Englishmen. With Sir Walter Raleigh's raiding exploits on gold-laden Spanish ships and with Shakespeare's immortalizing of the language, Englishmen came to think of themselves as subjects of something more than the sovereign. Perhaps this early national consciousness made it possible for Englishmen to see the monarch in his proper place, as Burke says, as the "basis" for government and not as the government itself; and this concept made it possible for the English to hold on to monarchy and to move at the same time toward parliamentary government.

It would be fruitless to speculate at this point as to whether Paine was more English than French in his concept of nationalism, but his writing reveals that he did conceive of the nation as an abstraction. The nation, he said, "is like a body contained within a circle, having a common center in which every radius meets; and that center is formed by representation" (I, 372). Moreover, in order to "clear away the rubbish of errors, into which the subject of government has been thrown" (I, 369), Paine unequivocally outlines the advantages of a republican form of government in order to show its superiority in every instance to monarchy. He begins with a definition of the term: "Republican government is no other than government established and conducted for the interest of the public, as well individually as collectively. It is not necessarily connected with any particular form, but it most naturally associates with the representative form, as being best calculated to secure the end for which a nation is at the expense of supporting it" (I, 370). Paine brings his examination to a close by again attacking monarchy as a mode of government which counteracts nature. The representative system, on the other hand, he views as being "always parallel with the order and immutable laws of nature" (I, 374).

If Paine could have foreseen the abuses of power that took place in Republican France during the Reign of Terror, he might have been embarrassed. He envisioned a government that delegates power for the benefit of society, promotes peace as a means of enriching the nation, sponsors universal society as a means of universal commerce, and proves its excellence by the small quantity of taxes required. But one year after France became a republic (September 1792) a handful of dedicated Jacobins, led by the now famous Maximillian Robespierre, instituted a Reign of Terror (1793–94) under the most dictatorial, war-minded, and chauvinistic government France has ever known. In addition, the revolutionary government never solved the financial problems of the country. When this Reign of Terror took place, Paine did not give up his ideas; he gave up France and came back to America.

*On Constitutions.* It may well be that Paine, an English commoner reared on a small island geographically isolated from the Continent, found it easier to think in abstract terms about a nation of people than did Sieyés, a nobleman who grew up as a subject of the supposedly absolute monarch, Louis XV. But Sieyés, although he was reluctant to give up the monarchy, proved to be an habitual constitution writer throughout the revolution, the Directory, and into the Napoleonic era. Consequently, Paine's thinking on constitutions is much more accurately contrasted to that of Burke. In fact, Paine adds very little about the theory of constitutions to what he had already said in his previous attacks on Burke. In part I, he clearly denounced the Burkean metaphysical concept of constitution and stated categorically that only written constitutions are the true ones; he repeats the same argument and proceeds, using the American constitution as a model, to define how constitutions should work.

Paine opens by differentiating between a constitution and a government. "A constitution," he says, "is not the act of a government, but of a people constituting a government; and government without a constitution, is power without a right" (I, 375). He illustrates this difference by briefly describing the processes by which a state constitution — that of Pennsylvania — and the Federal Constitution were formed. When the 1781 Act of Confederation was found to be inadequate (the powers of the states were found to be too great and those of the federal government too little), a second constitutional convention was convened in 1787, a new constitution was drafted, duly ratified, and implemented by the states. Paine then summarizes significantly the roles of the constitution and the government: "A constitution is the property of the nation, and not of those who exercise the government...." It "is a thing antecedent to the government, and always distinct therefrom" (I, 381).

To Paine, Englishmen have never understood, however, the difference between a constitution and a government. He tries to account for the widespread belief that such a thing as an English constitution does exist. The Magna Carta, he says, instead of creating and giving powers to a government as a constitution does, did no more than limit the powers of the existing government. The Bill of Rights, too, was no more than a compromise which the different parts of the government "made with each other to divide powers, profits, and privileges." It should be called a "bill of wrongs," Paine concludes. Because England has no constitution, many of her laws are irrational and tyrannical; and she places far too much reliance on precedent as a means of determining present policy (I, 383).

Paine next considers the constituent parts of a constitution. He points out that a nation has a right to establish a constitution, that it must consider for what ends the government is necessary and what are the best means of accomplishing these ends at the least expense. He continues with an analysis of the two divisions of power in civil government — the legislative and the executive. The one enacts laws and the other administers them (I, 387–88). From this analysis Paine moves to the organization of the legislative power, which, he says, should be wholly by representation in one or two houses. Taking note of the objections to a system of one and two houses, he proposes the following: (a) to have but one representation; (b) to divide that representation, by lots, into two or three parts; (c) to debate every proposed bill, by succession, in each part. Then the whole representation assembles for general debate and determination by vote (I, 390).

No one government individual would have such power that his sudden withdrawal — by death or incapacitating illness — would occasion disorder or confusion in the ongoing process of government. Furthermore, any individual in government who is given great power and extraordinary pay would become a center "round which every kind of corruption generates and dorms" (I, 392). For this reason, every department of the government should be decently provided for but no one should be paid extravagant wages. Relative to oaths of allegiance, Paine says that one should take an oath of allegiance to the nation only and not to a personality, like a king, for "putting any individual as a figure for a nation is improper" (I, 395).

Paine concludes by observing that in America provision has been made to alter the Constitution if the need arises, for "the best constitution that could now be devised, consistent with the condition of the present moment, may be far short of that excellence which a few years may afford" (I, 396–97).

*Ways and Means of Improving the Condition of Europe Interspersed with Miscellaneous Observations.* Whereas Paine in previous chapters had been preoccupied with disputing Burke and with proving the supremacy of representative republicanism over hereditary monarchy, he is concerned in this section with explaining in detail the procedure for implementing his proposed plan of government. France had established a legislative assembly but, so far, neither France nor England had gone so far as to change their forms of government from a limited monarchy to a republic; moreover, his suggestions are directives to all governments in Europe and occasionally rise to the level of humanitarianism and internationalism.

After a cursory attack upon English charters and corporations, the House of Peers, and the crown — all of which Paine sees as unnecessary to a well-functioning state — he defines the objective of government as the promotion of general happiness. In order to accomplish this aim, the poor, the aged, and the young must be given attention by the state. Four pounds a year should be provided for each child under the age of fourteen of poor parents in order to provide them with sufficient schooling to acquire skills in reading, writing, and basic arithmetic. Also, Paine's government would provide funds to educate children of parents "who, though, not properly of the class of poor, yet find it difficult to give education to their children" (I, 428). Every person over the age of fifty should receive an annual pension of six pounds; and, when he reaches sixty, the sum should be increased to ten pounds a year. "This support," claims Paine, "is not of the nature of charity, but of a right" (I, 427). The state would provide workhouses to which any indigent person might come, the only condition being that he work a required number of hours for his food and lodging. Other socialistic interests included funeral expenses of persons who "travelling for work, may die at a distance from their friends," and a cash payment of twenty shillings to every needy woman immediately on the birth of a child (I, 429).

Where did Paine expect to obtain the finances to make all these benefits available? He expected an alliance between England and France to result in a reduction in expenses for the army and the navy. The money thus saved could pay for the proposed benefits. In a more practical vein, he reexamined the bureaucratic standard of Britain and asserted that certain changes here would provide adequate funds to support the socialist measures he advocates. Proposed changes included the following: no man in government service to be paid beyond his services, which should never merit more than ten thousand pounds a year; abolition of primogeniture and a progressive taxation on property; the interest on the national debt considered as property, its interest to be taxed by some progressive ration; public taxes lessened in the same proportion as the interest diminished; elimination of taxes on houses and windows to benefit the middle class. These measures, Paine believed, would increase the amount of taxes paid by the wealthy and proportionately decrease the amount paid by the rest of society. Consequently, Paine's socialism would be supported in the main by those who were most able to pay for its support.

# CHAPTER 4

# *Reaction to Organized Religion*

T HE British government had remained relatively undisturbed concerning part I of *Rights of Man,* but part II, when it was published in England in February 1792, created a furor. Because Paine's forthright denouncement of the British monarchy reached a large segment of the poorer people whom the government feared might start a revolution, Prime Minister Pitt undertook a smear campaign against the character of Paine and initiated court action which eventually resulted in the libel conviction. In spite of and partly because of these distressing events, Paine's reputation was on the increase in France. Having been elected a representative from Calais to the National Convention on September 6, 1792, he left England six days later to assume his delegated duties.

The new representatives to the National Convention met in Paris on September 22, 1792, the first day of the first year of the new revolutionary calendar. On that very day, France was declared a republic; and Paine's dreams were at least in part fulfilled. Within the Convention, the monarchists were out of favor; and the Girondin party, long known for its advocacy of a republican government, was in power. But in the wings stood Robespierre, the most notorious of the radical Jacobins, who was determined to see the revolution become more radical — even to the point of forcing a Utopian state upon the people by arbitrary rule.

During the days of Girondin rule, with Jacobins pressuring France further and further toward the Reign of Terror, Paine's true sentiments about the French government became evident. When Louis XVI was brought to trial in France one month after Paine's trial in England, Paine's reaction to the trial marks a turning point in his revolutionary activities. His eloquent attempt to save the life of the king left Paine with his humanitarian principles unchanged but with few friends among the powerful Jacobin leaders who were to rule France for the next year.

About the issue of the king's treason, no substantial disagreement occurred; but, when it came to a matter of his execution, factions developed within the Convention. Girondists wanted to allow the French people to decide the monarch's fate in a popular referendum; Jacobin leaders favored execution; and royalists, of course, supported the king. Expressing characteristic independence, Paine followed no party line; he wanted the king held in prison and finally banished after the conclusion of the war. According to Aldridge, no one in the Convention worked harder to save the king's life than Paine;[1] but in the end the vote was 387 to 334; and Louis was led to the guillotine on January 21, 1793. With an air of dignity previously not expressed and with almost a sense of relief, it seems, this vacillating, reluctant king met his death. The execution was a tragic time for Paine, for he had pled eloquently before the Convention: "Kill the monarchy but save the king." In the end, however, neither of Paine's admonitions were to be heeded: Louis Capet was killed, and the Bourbons were later restored to the throne after the fall of Napoleon Bonaparte.

The king's execution was a shock to Paine's naïve belief in the natural goodness of mankind. To Paine, the advocacy of revolution meant the destruction of an oppressive government so that reasonable men might fashion a new world. He had witnessed something similar to this in America after the Revolution, but the French seemed to be throwing reason to the wind. Throughout the trial, Paine called for humanitarian concern; but he also argued reasonably that the execution of Charles I in England had not brought an end to the monarchy there; for the young pretender to the throne, Charles II, had returned from exile eleven years later to be restored to the throne. Similarly, Louis XVI had two younger brothers in exile who might become pretenders to the throne; moreover, they might secure the help of foreign monarchs, who were always threatened by the execution of any crowned head. Louis could find sanctuary in the United States and learn there the lessons of true government. More importantly, as long as Louis lived, there could be no pretender to the throne of France. In this manner Paine concluded his argument from reason. Nevertheless, Robespierre and Jean Paul Marat, the most influential leaders of the Convention, disregarded all consideration of the dignity of mankind, and a majority of the representatives followed them.

Paine now experienced disillusionment for the first time, and his thoughts turned to religion. This move was not just a sentimental search for personal comfort; he had already noticed that, just as attacks upon government had led to inhumane considerations, so attacks upon religion were leading to atheism. As early as the summer of 1793, with the Reign of Terror in full swing, Paine abandoned hope that liberty, equality, and fraternity would be spread to the nations of Europe; actualization of these ideas was in doubt even in France. With his Jacobin enemies in power and his own life in danger, Paine turned his attentions to the writing of *The Age of Reason*.

## I   *Part First*

In his opening statement Paine, fearing that his work might not see the light of day in France, places it under the protection of his "fellow citizens of the United States"; and he makes it clear that his "formidable weapon" in the ensuing work will be "reason" (I, 463). Having seen revolution effected in America and France, Paine reveals his conviction that these political revolutions will probably result in a revolution in the system of religion. Since his political vision was by now enlarged to encompass world revolution, there is no reason to doubt that Paine expected to see a world-wide revolution in religion.

He professes disbelief in the creeds of all churches — Jewish, Roman, Greek, Turkish, and Protestant. In case he has overlooked any, Paine declares his inability to believe in "any church that I know of," for "my own mind is my own church," he affirms (I, 464). He speaks boldly against institutionalized religion, which was set up, he claims, "to terrify and enslave mankind," and against priests, who are guilty of "mental lying," or hypocrisy, which he describes as the root of all crime. In contrast, Paine praises the "chastity" of the "mind" and describes true religion as the product of the "mind of man" communicating with itself: "I believe in one God and no more; and I hope for happiness beyond this life. I believe in the equality of man; and I believe that religious duties consist in doing justice, loving mercy, and endeavoring to make our fellow-creatures happy" (I, 464).

Since Paine professed to believe in Deism, we must interpret his profession of faith against the background of Deistic, not orthodox, Christian belief. Consequently, we must place Deism in its historical context in order to understand Paine's religious views and those of the eighteenth century in general. The most important single event at the beginning of the eighteenth century was the discovery of the law of gravity by Sir Isaac Newton. After Newton's discovery, many thinking men sought to discover similar simple and general Newtonian Laws which would reveal the secrets of the universe in areas other than the physical sciences. Adam Smith in *Wealth of Nations* (1776), who advocated *laissez-faire* doctrines, advised that the way for a country to become economically wealthy was to remove all governmental regulations and restrictions upon trade. Rousseau discovered the Newtonian Law of government simply to be "rule by the people." In the area of religion, application of scientific thought produced Deism, which was based upon the simple hypothesis that God created the universe, hurled it into space, and allowed it to operate according to the laws of nature. This concept became known as the Watchmaker God: A Newtonian Law of religion. On the basis of this fundamental belief, the *philosophes* examined religious doctrines and practices. However, most of them were content to point out only glaring inconsistencies between belief and practice, such as religious persecution carried out by supposed apostles of love and peace; and, unlike Paine, they disdained to propagandize this new religion, especially among the unlearned.

Paine proposes to deal with two matters initially in part I: (1) a rejection of "revelation" as interpreted by institutionalized religion as the basis of all true and superior knowledge; and (2) advocacy of a "new revelation," which is reason. After briefly stating his own Deist profession of faith, he proceeds to the first of the two issues.

Possibly because the church had kept alive the dichotomy, Paine seems to have been aware of the division of knowledge established by Scholastics of the late Middle Ages such as St. Anselm, Peter Abelard, and Thomas Aquinas. All of these men talked about two kinds of knowledge — one which man figures out for himself: and one which is revealed to him by God through the church and the scriptures. St. Anselm set the pace for the Scholastics in his *Cur Deus Homo,* in which he clearly showed how man could, through philosophical inquiry, arrive at proof for the existence of God. This proof is as far, however, as man's mind could go, for superior knowledge that goes beyond just belief in God's existence must come from God through revelation. Other Scholastics continued to talk about the difference between natural theology and divine knowledge until Aquinas declared in his *Summa Theologica* that no conflict exists between the two kinds of knowledge since both seek the same truth.

*On Revelation.* To Paine, "revelation when applied to religion, means something communicated *immediately* from God to man." While he does not deny that this revelation could have happened and created the scriptures of various religions, what was revelation became "hearsay" when the church passed down these revealed truths to succeeding generations (I, 465–66). His rejection, then, of the church's notion that revealed knowledge is superior to any other knowledge leads him to an examination of the many ways in which this revealed knowledge developed and was transmitted through the ages; and he included the central figure in the Christian revelation, Jesus Christ.

*Jesus Christ and His Mission.* Paine accepted historical evidence that Jesus Christ existed and was crucified as "strictly within the limits of probability" (I, 469). But, as to the supernatural part of the story of Jesus, including his virgin birth and his resurrection, this claim "has every mark of fraud and imposition stamped upon the face of it" (I, 468). Although we can hardly describe Paine as a philosopher, we can say that his description of Christ is a renunciation of the Scholastics' concept of revealed truth. Paine simply refuses to accept the virgin birth as truth although the church had declared it to be revealed truth. At the same time, he reveals an influence traceable to the famous seventeenth-century French philosopher, René Descartes, who was one of the great forerunners of the Enlightenment and one of the founders of the French philosophical school known as Rationalism. Descartes's influence upon the men of the Enlightenment was probably as great as Newton's, for both men opened up new worlds of ideas to those who came after them.

Descartes's works were revolutionary because he made deductive reasoning boundless. Whereas Anselm had set out to prove deductively that God does exist, Descartes assumed only that he, Descartes, existed and proceeded to deduce an extensive philosophy from that hypothesis. Paine, like Voltaire and other *philosophes* influenced by Descartes, applied reason to religion; but he remained a Deist. On the other hand, a number of late eighteenth-century *philosophes* and other writers were more influenced by the materialistic implications of Descartes's work than was Paine. La Mettrie, author of *Man a Machine,* and Denis Diderot, editor of the famous *Encyclopedia* — a collection of writings by *philosophes* and others — are but two of a number of influential thinkers who had already moved beyond Deism to materialism before the French Revolution began and who were asking why the Deist's Watchmaker God was necessary. Furthermore, during the fall of 1793, when Paine wrote most of the work on part I of *The Age of Reason,* the French government closed the churches and made a strong effort to eradicate Catholicism and to substitute a state religion of reason in its place. While Paine had made a solid break with the medieval past, he was not ready to discard belief in God. He is writing not only to halt the spread of atheism but also to confound every priest who would "subscribe his professional belief to things he does not believe" (I, 465).

Paine may not have realized the philosophical implications of his views, but the works of John Locke were a part of the intellectual setting that influenced all the *philosophes* and Paine. If Descartes liberated modern man from medieval inhibitions to reasoning, John Locke introduced him to the importance of experience. According to Locke, knowledge of our existence is intuitive and comes to us from our experience. When we add to the importance of Locke's emphasis on experience the empirical emphasis of Newton's discovery, there is little wonder that Paine accepted the natural part of the story of Jesus, subject to verification by repetition, and rejected the supernatural part which could not be verified by personal experience and repetition. Paine might go to Jerusalem or even die on a cross as Jesus did, but he could not ascend to heaven. All those things which could not be verified by repetition, Paine termed unnatural.

In the next three sections — *Fabulous Bases of Christianity, Examination of the Preceding Bases,* and *Of the True Theology* — Paine brands the doctrine of the "cross" (God's sacrificing himself in the crucifixion of Jesus) as unnatural. If the "Christian Mythologists" had had Satan (the Spirit of Evil) die upon the cross, this death would have been natural; but "the more unnatural anything is, the more it is capable of becoming the object of dismal admiration" (I, 471). It was because Jesus was a "virtuous reformer and revolutionist [that he] lost his life," proclaimed Paine (I, 469), not because tragedy was written into the order of nature as was indicated by the church's doctrine of the "sacrifice of the Creator."

In contrast to the dismal doctrine of the cross, Paine makes public his belief in the benevolence of nature, a characteristic doctrine of the eighteenth-century *philosophes*. He speaks of "a fair creation prepared to receive us the instant we are born," and he talks about the "blessings" afforded by "the vast machinery of the universe" (I, 472). As a consolation to men who are troubled by the church's mournful and unnatural theology, Paine moves to an examination of the Old and New Testaments.

*Examination of the Old Testament.* The Bible is not the word of God, according to Paine. The word of God would have to be unchangeable and carry with it "the utter impossibility of any change taking place, by any means or accident." Therefore, "the word of God cannot exist in any written or human language" (I, 477); and many modern scholars concur with this view absolutely. They point to the Greek word "logos" in John 1:1 which is inaccurately translated as "word" in the King James Version of the Bible, and they emphasize that it might be better translated "the spirit holding the universe together."[2]

Paine was ahead of his time when he ridiculed the manner whereby books were chosen to be contained in the Bible. It was by majority vote of church councils that some books were included and others excluded from the Bible. Not incidentally, although Paine does not mention it specifically, the Council of Nicaea in A.D. 325 decided on the doctrine of the Trinity by majority vote. In this light, Paine's scathing indictment takes on added force: "Had they voted otherwise, —all the people, since calling themselves Christians, had believed otherwise — for the belief of the one comes from the vote of the other" (I, 473).

Speaking of the Old Testament alone, Paine rejects the Mosaic authorship of the Book of Genesis, describes the Psalms and Job as "no higher rank than many other compositions on similar subjects," considers Proverbs as "inferior ... to the proverbs of the Spaniards, and not more wise and economical than those of the American Franklin," and levels the devastating charge that the Old Testament prophets were no more than poets (I, 474–75). Writing from memory, Paine parenthetically says that in the Book of Job "we find a great deal of elevated sentiment reverentially expressed of the power and benignity of the Almighty" (I, 474). Job, who waited patiently to hear the voice of God, seems to have impressed Paine more than any other character in the Old Testament.

*Of the New Testament.* The approach here is similar to that employed in criticizing the Old Testament. Denying things supernatural while emphasizing the moral and ethical teachings of the books, Paine rejects the divinity of Christ while extolling his philanthropy (I, 478). In this section, Paine makes absurd remarks, and one of them is his denial of the saving power of the cross on the grounds that "men die faster since the crucifixion than before." This statement, along with the caustic remark about St. Paul's being a "manufacturer of quibbles," makes it easy to understand some of the bitterness his writings created among biblical scholars (I, 479). A much more substantive and meaningful attack, however, is contained in his accusation that the church on the basis of the New Testament books "has set up a system of religion very contradictory to the character of the person whose name it bears" (I, 480). Paine's rejection of the scholastic concept of revelation led him to offer a new approach to revealed knowledge.

*The New Revelation.* Until this point, Paine has employed an almost exclusively negative approach while attempting to discredit the Bible as an agent of revelation. He then turns to a positive affirmation of a new revelation and the consequences of it in *The True Revelation* and *True Theology,* for Paine lays the foundation for all that he will say in the rest of part I. His thesis is that God is revealed through the laws of nature. "Yes, there is a word of God; there is a revelation," proclaims Paine; for God speaks to man through "THE CREATION WE BEHOLD" (I, 482).

Paine does not express the teachings of Pantheism like those espoused by the seventeenth-century philosopher Baruch Spinoza, who thought of mind and matter as aspects of God. To Paine, God was not the same as the universe but was the "first cause" of it. He also sought to repudiate atheists who maintained that the universe had always existed. Man "arrives at the belief ... [in a first cause] from the tenfold greater difficulty of disbelieving it." The universe "carries in itself the internal evidence that it did not make itself" (I, 484). In fact, Paine is really putting forth an argument somewhat similar to that of St. Anselm, who believed that one could by reason prove the existence of God, but that further knowledge of God comes through revelation.

At the same time, Paine's views differed markedly from Anselm's about the issue of the agent of revelation. God's attributes were, according to Paine, revealed not through the church or the scriptures but through nature. Yet, he found only three instances in the Bible of what he terms "natural religion." Several chapters in Job and the 19th Psalm, Paine says, "treat of the *Deity* through his works" (I, 484); and in the New Testament, Jesus admonished: "Behold the lilies of the field, they toil not,neither do they spin" (I, 486). Still, Paine finds many evidences outside the Bible of God's revelation through nature, and the foremost of these agents of revelation is science.

To Paine, true theoogy is the study of science, or the laws or principles of science, for they are of "divine origin" and God seeks "to teach" man through these laws (I, 489–90). Through the new theology Paine seeks to counteract atheism and materialism. There is even a hint of Theism (belief in a personal God who is concerned about mankind) in his description of God as the "Almighty Lecturer" (I, 490); and, Paine insists — just as do adherents of idealism (the opposite of materialism) — that ideas exist independently of matter: "All the properties of a triangle exist independently of the figure, and existed before any triangle was drawn or thought of by man" (I, 488).

*Education and History.* Paine broadens the scope of his animosity toward medieval concepts to include the "Renaissance Spirit" of learning wherein scholars found the study of ancient languages, especially Greek, to have meaning within itself. "It would be advantageous to the state of learning to abolish the study of dead languages," Paine writes (I, 492). Although "almost all the scientific learning that now exists came to us from the Greeks," all the useful books in the Greek language have been translated (I, 491); and "it is only in the living languages that new knowledge is to be found." Learning today should consist, "as it originally did, in scientific knowledge" (I, 492), as was the case with ancient Greece.

In this respect, Paine was a true son of the Enlightenment, for he regarded Greek civilization as the greatest achievement up to that time in history. However, contributions by Greek poets, who emphasized tragedy as an integral part of life, were unappreciated by Paine. Eventually there would be a revival of interest in this aspect of the Greek heritage, but it would not come about until the nineteenth century. That Paine's typical eighteenth-century belief in progress left no room for a sense of tragedy is evident in his complete misunderstanding of the theological implications of the doctrine of the cross. To Paine, "the corporal idea of the death of a god" was an "outrage to the moral justice of God" (I, 492–93). Inhibited by the restrictions of eighteenth-century Rationalism, Paine allows himself to appear to dictate to God the terms of divine moral justice. The personal tragedy he suffered during the Reign of Terror, when he was writing *The Age of Reason,* may have turned Paine toward a consideration of religion, but it never became a part of his ideas about religion.

In summary, Paine viewed the medieval and Renaissance periods as an interregnum between the reigns of Greek Reason and the Reason of the seventeenth and eighteenth centuries. "If we take our stand about the beginning of the sixteenth century," he writes, "we look back through that long chasm to the times of the ancients, as over a vast, sandy desert, in which not a shrub appears to intercept the vision to the fertile hills beyond." With the appearance of Martin Luther and the Protestant Reformation in the early sixteenth century, "the sciences began to revive," but this revival, according to Paine, was the only good the Reformation accomplished. "The mythology still continued the same," and Paine decries the fact that "National Popes grew out of the downfall of the Age of Christendom" (I, 495).

Paine's assessment of medieval society appears to us simplistic: a people completely submissive to papal control. Although the Roman Church sought to control education and to prevent objective inquiry throughout the Middle Ages, recent scholarship has shown evidences of anticlericalism long before A.D. 1500. In addition to literary attacks upon the excesses of the clergy by such literary lights as Chaucer and Dante, there were also violent outbursts against the clergy, especially against the Franciscans, because of their lack of concern for the suffering of people in the period after the Black Death in the sixteenth century.

If Paine's characterization of the age of Chaucer and Dante as one devoid of any element of modernity is difficult to understand, then his lumping of fifteenth-century Italian Renaissance figures into the same category is incredible. In a sense, Paine is on safe ground in choosing A.D. 1500 as the date when the links "in the long chain of despotic ignorance" (I, 495) began to break. Copernicus published his revolutionary heliocentric theories about the universe as late as 1543, and his work is accepted by many as the beginning of the scientific revolution. However, for Paine to assume that nothing of any importance to modern science happened in the preceding century is to overlook Leonardo da Vinci's keen observations of nature and his many scientific experiments. And before da Vinci came Giotto, whose works are generally recognized as a bridge between medieval and Renaissance art, and Masaccio, who created a revolution in painting by the application of mathematical laws of perspective. Any such theory of the gradual evolution of history would have been meaningless to Paine, however, for he interpreted history as the story of abrupt revolution.

In the next two sections, Paine continues the theme of the New Revelation by relating it to his knowledge of astronomy. He rejects the traditional Christian belief that "this world that we inhabit is the whole of the habitable creation," and he asserts that "there is room for millions of worlds as large or larger than ours" (I, 499–500). He gives a detailed description of our solar system and extrapolates from this one system of worlds an immense space filled with many "systems of worlds" (I, 502). "The inhabitants of each of the worlds of which our system is composed enjoy the same opportunities of knowledge as we do: They behold the revolutionary motion of our earth, as we behold theirs." Since "knowledge of science is derived from the revolutions (exhibited to our eye and from thence to our understanding)" (I, 503), all inhabitants of a "plurality of worlds" are instructed by the same Creator.

There are monistic implications in Paine's description of a plurality of worlds in which "no part of space lies at waste" (I, 502–503), but one feature that distinguishes this from Pantheism is the insistence on God as the Creator who through nature (movement of the planets) instructs the inhabitants of all the worlds. At any rate, Paine's primary purpose in this section is to debunk the notion that God would disregard the care of all other worlds and "come to die in our world" through the sacrifice of his son.

*Mystery, Miracle, and Prophecy.* Paine speaks of "three principal means that have been employed in all ages, perhaps in all countries, to impose upon mankind" — mystery, miracle, and prophecy (I, 505). Paine sees all three as crutches that should be rejected by the one religion that is true — that is, natural religion, or religion as revealed through nature. In this section, Paine ridicules the story of Jonah and the whale: "It would have approached nearer to the idea of a miracle if Jonah had swallowed the whale," Paine writes skeptically (I, 509). But perhaps the sharpest mockery he delivered to Christian apologists of his day was his sarcastic description of the flight of Jesus and the Devil through the air "to the top of the highest pinnacle of the temple." Paine asks, "How happened it that he did not discover America?" (I, 509). Paine may or may not have been aware that the New Testament stated that the purpose of this flight was for Satan to show and to offer the kingdoms of the world to Jesus. At any rate, to associate such a moral lesson with so mundane a matter as the discovery of the New World was to incur the antagonism of devout Christians.

Paine continues to recapitulate his major intentions. He denounces the Bible as the word of God, and he offers a new word of God — a new revelation that comes through nature. Finally, he insists that man's moral duty "consists in imitating the moral goodness and beneficence of God, manifested in our creation toward all his creations" (I, 512). Deism, he says, is the true religion, but every man has a right to the religion he prefers.

## II   *Part Second*

On December 28, 1793, when Paine finished writing part I, he was almost immediately placed under arrest. Having known for some time that he was out of favor with the Committee of Public Safety, the arbitrary governing body of France headed by Robespierre, Paine had written part I with the expectation of being arrested and possibly executed. After nearly a year in prison, Paine was released and taken into the home of James Monroe, American minister to Paris and later President of the United States. Here he recuperated from a prison illness and set about composing part II of *The Age of Reason.*

In the brief preface Paine declares that this work is not a deliberate answer to those writers who have criticized part I; but he states later on that, since his critics have attacked him upon the basis of the Holy Scriptures and since he now has access to a copy of the same,[3] "I will therefore come on their own ground, and oppose them with their own weapon, the Bible" (I, 521).

*The Word of God.* In part I, Paine had declared that "the Bible is not the word of God." Here he argues the same point in greater detail and attacks the traditional authorship of certain books accredited to Moses, Joshua, and Samuel in order to nullify their claim to authenticity. Viewed in this light, these early books become nothing but "stories, fables and traditionary or invented absurdities," declares Paine. In some cases, he continues, they are filled with downright lies (I, 528).

Paine's attack on the Mosaic authorship of the Pentateuch, the first five books in the Old Testament, poses no threat to modern biblical scholarship; for, since the Darwinian revolution of the nineteenth century and the resulting strife between religion and science, scholars have been forced either to apply critical methods to the authorship of books in the Bible or to restrict themselves to a narrow fundamentalism. Still, Paine was far ahead of his time in pointing out that these books were written long after Moses' time in history; and to make this claim then was to challenge a popularly held belief.

Paine appears as a true forerunner of the late nineteenth-century practitioners of biblical criticism when he points out that the city called "Dan" in Genesis "was not called Dan until 331 years after the death of Moses" (I, 526) and also when he points to "facts done after the death of Joshua" as evidence that these books could not have been written by Moses and Joshua. However, when he describes the Old Testament as "a book of lies, wickedness and blasphemy" (I, 529), he reveals his lack of objectivity. Moreover, it becomes abundantly clear that, unlike later critics who sought objectively to discover both from internal and external evidence just when and by whom books in the Bible were written, Paine basically felt that the Bible is untrue.

Modern scholars decline to name one author for the Pentateuch or for any of the early books in the Bible. A rather general view is that Genesis began as oral history out of which some written documents based upon various traditional stories appeared. Finally, the various written accounts, such as $J_1$, $J_2$, E, *et cetera,* were compiled into one book. Something of the same procedure also took place with regard to all the early books of the Old Testament and the New Testament. Although Kings and Chronicles and similar accounts do not fall into this category, their authors had access to many and

varied sources, and the very human element of editorial work frequently resulted in errors.

Paine relied on internal and external evidence to discredit the
Bible. He observed that the account in Joshua of the sun standing
still "is one of those fables that detects itself." On the basis of
external evidence, he argues that this was the type of event that
would certainly have been noticed and recorded universally, yet no
other people except the Jews "know anything about it" (I, 532). As
to the internal evidence, Joshua and Judges, he says, because of the
similarity of style are the work of the same author (I, 536). Judges
and the two books of Samuel are anonymous, but the "idle,
bungling story, foolishly told ... about a strolling country-girl,
creeping slyly to bed with her cousin Booz [*sic*]" (I, 535) is enough
within itself to prove it is not the word of God.

Paine's treatment of the two books of Kings and of the two
books of Chronicles is designed to show contradictions between
these accounts and those found elsewhere. Also, he was intent on
revealing the extreme cruelty of God's "chosen people." A classic
example often referred to is the incident in which a "parcel of children [called] Elisha *bald head, bald head,* and ... this *Man of God*
... 'Turned back, and looked on them, *and cursed them in the
name of the Lord,* and there came forth two she-bears out of the
wood, and tore forty-and-two children of them'" (I, 541).

In his treatment of the book of Ezra, Paine very astutely calls
attention to an editorial error. The author of Chronicles breaks off
abruptly in the middle of a sentence. The phrase "Let him go up"
in Chronicles becomes "let him go up to Jerusalem" in Ezra (I,
544). Paine views this error as evidence of "disorder and ignorance"; later biblical scholars were to term it "poor editorial work."

The book of Esther is considered anonymous and, to Paine, of
no consequence. But the book of Job "differs in character from all
the books we have hitherto passed over" (I, 547). It speaks well of
Paine's memory and of his integrity as a reporter that in part I,
without having a Bible for reference, he had already set the book of
Job apart as different from the rest of the Old Testament. Now he
reaffirms this opinion, referring to two Hebrew commentators,
Abenezra (Ibnezra), a fourteenth-century Spanish scholar, and
Spinoza, who said that Job definitely was not a Hebrew book but
was a product of Gentile culture (I, 547).

All of Psalms were not the work of King David, according to

Paine (I, 549); and most modern scholars would agree. Only seventy-three of the one hundred fifty Psalms are by the Bible attributed to David; however, in Paine's time it was thought that David had written all the Psalms. Paine also perceived from internal evidence that parts of two chapters in Isaiah "could only have been written by some person who lived at least a hundred and fifty years after Isaiah was dead" (I, 553). It is possible, but not probable, that Paine got the idea from Abenezra, who expressed doubts about Isaiah's authorship of chapters 40–66. Paine has earlier relied upon the authority of Abenezra, but in this case, he, unlike Abenezra, refers only to the forty-fourth and forty-fifth chapters. The twelfth-century Hebrew scholar was more perceptive than Paine, for there is widespread agreement among scholars today that large portions of Isaiah came from other authors, especially chapters 40–66.

Proverbs came "from authors belonging to other nations than those of the Jewish nation." Ecclesiastes was probably written by Solomon; but Paine, who sees no virtue in this fact, describes Solomon as "a worn-out debauche" who was "miserable in his old age" (I, 550–51), and he contrasts him to Benjamin Franklin, who maintained a youthful mind until his death (I, 551).

Having already described the Hebrew prophets as no more than mere poets, Paine reaffirms this opinion and ridicules the idea that Isaiah's statement "Behold a virgin shall conceive, and bear a son" (I, 553) was a prophecy of Mary and Jesus. The statement was no more than the promise of a sign to King Ahaz, King of Judah, that the kings of Syria and Israel would not make war upon them. For Isaiah to make this prediction come true would be simple since it would not be difficult to "find a girl with child." The story, says Paine, "has no more reference to Christ and his mother than it has to me and my mother" (I, 554).

The other prophets are described as being equally crafty in making safe predictions. Moreover, much of what has come to be thought of as prophecy was really ordinary information intentionally written so as to hide its meaning from enemies. Paine draws a ludicrous picture of biblical scholars "wasting their time in pretending to expound and unriddle" (I, 564) what they thought to be pertinent prophesies. For example, the famous statement from Ezekiel about "a wheel within a wheel" relates to the time of Ezekiel and refers to "political contrivance" whereby Jerusalem would be recovered from enemies (I, 565). In the light of modern biblical scholarship, Paine's explanation is too simplistic. The history of the book of Ezekiel has been so complicated that definitive statements about its meaning have to be considered as no more than probability. But Paine was not writing to modern scholars; rather, his message was to eighteenth-century priests and ordinary people who saw in Ezekiel's imagery prophecies of things to come.

*The New Testament.* In comparison to the Old Testament, the New Testament, because of its brevity, "is like a farce of one act," says Paine, "in which there is not room for very numerous violations of the unities" (I, 571). However, he has uncovered some "glaring contradictions" on the basis of which he seeks to discredit the New Testament as the word of God. After an opening thrust at the obvious difference between the genealogical accounts of Christ given by Matthew and Luke, Paine proceeds, using a method similar to that employed in his treatment of the books of the Old Testament, to cast doubt upon the validity of the gospels of Matthew, Mark, Luke, and John. In contrast to his treatment of the Old Testament, he now finds it sufficient to show that there are too many inconsistencies between the accounts for them to have been written by eyewitnesses. Since the traditional authors of the gospel were supposed to have been eyewitnesses, it follows logically that they were not the authors.

*Inconsistencies and Contradictions Between the Four Gospel Accounts.* Paine itemizes the following differences between the gospels. The story of the virgin birth of Mary, the mother of Christ, is not mentioned in either Mark or John, and the accounts given by Matthew and Luke are different.[4] Matthew alone records the story of Herod's destroying all the children under two years of age (I, 574) and the account of the veil of the Temple being "rent in twain" (I, 575). "Not any two of these writers agree in reciting, exactly in the same words, the written inscription ... over Christ when he was crucified." Finally, Mark and John do not agree on the hour of crucifixion (I, 574–75).

Paine, who cites numerous differences in the various accounts of the resurrection, states that, if the writers of these four books had testified in a court of justice "in the same contradictory manner as it is here given, they would have been in danger of having their ears cropped for perjury, and would have justly deserved it" (I, 578). Paine marvels at the number of "glaring absurdities, contradictions and falsehoods" in these accounts which after all covered but a few days time between the crucifixion and the resurrection; moreover, all these circumstances were supposed to have taken place "about the same spot, Jerusalem" (I, 582).

As in the case of the Old Testament, the various accounts were probably passed down by word of mouth; but in this instance eye-witnesses contributed heavily to the oral tradition, something which cannot be said of the account of the creation recorded in Genesis. In light of this evidence, many modern Bible scholars would argue that the similarity in the accounts attests to the validity of the story of the resurrection; but Paine has an answer for them: "The story of Jesus Christ appearing after he was dead is the story of an apparition, such as timid imaginations can always create a vision, and credulity believe." Throughout history, there have been stories of the ghosts of any number of great men, notably Julius Caesar: "Once start a ghost and credulity fills up the history of its life and assigns the cause of its appearance" (I, 584). Still, according to Paine, the answer is to be found in the difference between "legendary tale" and "fact," and there is little doubt that Paine regards the latter as superior knowledge — perhaps the only knowledge. Paine then moves in the second part of this chapter to a consideration of the epistles of St. Paul.

*Epistles of St. Paul.* In the case of these writings, authorship "is a matter of no great importance, since the writer, whoever he was, attempts to prove his doctrine by argument," declares Paine. Unlike the authors of the gospels, Paul "does not pretend to have been witness to any of the scenes told of the resurrection and the ascension" (I, 590). Consequently, Paine considers most of what Paul wrote to be unworthy of consideration. Almost the entire section of "the Epistles of Paul" is devoted to an attack upon the fifteenth chapter of I Corinthians, in which Paul stated his ideas about the resurrection. Paine, if he had understood what he read, would have been greatly surprised at the similarity between his view and that of Paul.

Paine states categorically that "the doctrine ... [that Paul] sets out to prove by argument is the resurrection of the same body, and he advances this as an evidence of immortality" (I, 590). Paine obviously overlooked the clear-cut statement in the forty-fourth verse of the King James Version: "It is sown a natural body, it is raised a spiritual body." It is difficult to define exactly what Paul meant by this statement, but he clearly did not mean the resurrection of the same body that had died. Since some Palestinians did preach the resurrection of the same body, Paul's statement may have been an attempt to answer them.

Paine allows himself to be diverted by the apostle's metaphor of a grain of wheat which must die in the ground if it is to raise itself; and, when he counters with his own metaphor which he declares to be superior, he uses the caterpillar that evolves into a butterfly. Here, Paine declares, "everything is changed" (I, 592). In both cases, Paine and Paul were attempting to illustrate that for which there is no natural metaphor. Whereas Paul's statement is obviously an ill-conceived afterthought, the limitations of Paine's analogy are stated clearly in his description of the caterpillar as passing to a state "resembling" death (I, 592). Both men described what takes place in nature in an attempt to set forth what they believed about the resurrection. Both were — and had to be — poor illustrations.

For all practical purposes Paul gave up attempts to give an adequate rational or natural explanation. In the end, he somewhat mystically combined the two worlds, the physical and the spiritual, in the phrase "spiritual body." Paine might as well have given up. Although he believed that "the continuance of that consciousness of [existence] is immortality," he admitted that no one can say how "a thought is produced in what we call the mind" (I, 591).

Paine had charged Paul with advocating the resurrection "as evidence of immortality" (I, 590). It would be much more accurate to say that Paul had encountered the risen Christ on the Damascus Road and, as a result of this experience, believed in immortality. It was, then, his belief in immortality which led to his arguments about the resurrection and not the contrary, as Paine claimed. The same can be said of Paine, who experienced God in nature and allowed this to lead to his belief in immortality. In the end, Paine says the metaphor of the grain of wheat "shows Paul to have been what he says of others, a fool" (I, 593). Paul would perhaps say the same of Paine's analogy of the butterfly.

It is interesting to note that, as Paine concludes his arguments against the Bible, he seeks to disavow responsibility for what he set out to do. "Should the Bible⁵ and the New Testament hereafter fall, it is not I that have done it" (I, 594).

*Conclusion.* In his brief conclusion Paine takes a parting shot at the account of creation given in the book of Genesis: "They make there to have been three days and three nights, evenings and mornings, before there was a sun; when it is the presence or absence of the sun that is the cause of day and night" (I, 602), n. 26). Also singled out for a concluding volley is the Sermon on the Mount, especially the teaching regarding love for one's enemies. "The doctrine is hypocritical," exclaims Paine, "and it is natural that hypocrisy should act the reverse of what it preaches" (I, 598). Throughout history, he continues, Christians have been persecutors of those who disagree with them. "The only sect that has not persecuted are the Quakers" (I, 597), and the reason for this is that they are really Deists and not Christians. Deists, claims Paine, see God revealed in the works of his creation, and also in conscience (I, 596). This belief is as much religion as is needed; it is the only true religion (I, 600).

CHAPTER 5

# To Build a Better World: The Final Years

D URING the time that Paine was working on part II of *The Age of Reason,* he became increasingly restive. He was by temperament a revolutionist, and France, after Robespierre's fall, was enjoying a respite from revolution. Although more moderate men were in control, there were still occasions of disorder, such as the insurrection of François Babeuf, an early advocate of communist theories. Though he supported Babeuf's ideas, Paine deplored his violent methods.[1] Thus afforded an impetus, he codified his own program of social welfare in *Agrarian Justice,* his last significant work.

## I  *An End to Poverty*

Unlike Babeuf, Paine put forth his ideas in *Agrarian Justice* by "legitimate and constitutional means." The socialist ideas with which he had concluded *Rights of Man* take in this work the concrete form of specific methods for improving conditions in Europe. Specifically, Paine hoped that his plan to effect Socialism at the expense of the propertied class would become a reality in France, England, and America. To remove the appearance of communism from his equality of property proposal, Paine, in the "Author's Inscription to the Legislature and the Executive Directory of the French Republic," succinctly delineates two kinds of property: natural property, "that which comes to us from the Creator of the Universe," and artificial or acquired property, "the invention of men" (I, 606). He expresses belief in the equality of natural property, but he makes it clear he does not advocate equality of acquired property.

120

Paine explains in the "Author's English Preface" that it was Bishop Richard Watson's attack upon *The Age of Reason* that motivated him to write *Agrarian Justice.* Contradicting the Bishop, Paine states that "It is wrong to say God made *rich* and *poor;* He made only *male* and *female;* and He gave them the earth for their inheritance" (I, 609). The "noble savage" of North America, Paine writes, was in a natural state before the arrival of the white man, and in this state poverty was unknown. However, the effect of civilization was and is "to make one part of society more affluent, and the other more wretched" (I, 610). At this point, Paine states his thesis for *Agrarian Justice,* whose subject is "what the state of society ought to be": "The condition of every person born into the world, after a state of civilization commences, ought not to be worse than if he had been born before that period" (I, 610).

Paine does not advocate the collective ownership of property, as did the disciples of his contemporary, Comte de Saint-Simon; nor does he think it possible to retrogress "from the civilized to the natural state" (I, 610). At the same time, he asserts that in the natural, uncultivated state, the earth was "the common property of the human race," and "every proprietor, therefore, of cultivated lands, owes to the community a *ground-rent* (for I know of no better term to express the idea)" (I, 611). On the basis of this theory, Paine describes his plan to collect the *ground-rent* from the propertied class and to make it available to the poor, the sick, and the aged.

*Plan for Creating the Fund.* Using, for purposes of illustration, an estimate of the national capital of England for the year 1796, Paine outlines step-by-step a very detailed procedure for creating and distributing the fund. He reasons that the entire national capital will turn over by inheritance every thirty years; consequently, one may divide it by thirty to get the theoretical amount to pass to the next generation each year. An inheritance tax of ten percent of this figure to be paid by direct heirs and twenty percent to be paid by more distant heirs, he says, will produce a fund of 5,666,666 pounds for distribution annually. Four hundred thousand persons over fifty years of age will each receive ten pounds, ninety thousand persons who reach twenty-one will receive fifteen pounds, and 316,000 pounds will remain to be apportioned to the blind, the lame, and others unable to earn a living at a rate of ten pounds per year (I, 615–17).

Just as Paine has advocated revolution in government and religion, he now advocates a revolution in the economic state created by civilization. "It is not charity but a right," he states (I, 621). Many other writers of Paine's time, such as the English philosopher and socialist Jeremy Bentham, advocated the inheritance tax, but according to Samuel Edwards, the idea of providing state aid for the aged seems to have been original with Paine.[2] Thus far, however, Paine's suggestions have been purely hypothetical. Next, he moves to the practical matter of how the plan will work.

*Execution of the Plan.* Paine details in eight steps the procedure for establishing his fund. Beginning with the election of three persons in each canton who would be commissioned to carry out the collection of taxes, and carrying through to the second year of the plan, he surmises that the fund will support itself. Paine failed, however, to include in his estimates the necessary means to pay the salaries of commissioners, tax assessors, and an entire bureaucracy necessary to carry out such a plan. Although there are no doubt other more technical oversights, his plan was audacious and farsighted. Although it was considered revolutionary in his time, it has since been employed with some variation in many countries.

## II   *A Parting Shot at England*

Back in Paris in 1796, Paine published *The Decline and Fall of the English System of Finance,* which forecast a breakdown of the English funding system. Paine had previously pointed out in *Prospects on the Rubicon* that England's wealth had increased only in terms of paper currency. Here he carries the attack forward with an elaborate calculation of expense of past wars as a means of showing the progression of the funding system to destruction. The increasing depreciation of paper money is impossible to prevent, Paine writes, while the quantity of that money and of bank notes continues to multiply. The value of paper does not keep equal with the value of gold and silver; and, when the present quantity of cash is paid out by the bank, no means will be left for the bank to obtain a new supply.

The work was circulated widely at low cost in England and was immediately translated into French. Characteristically, Paine devoted all the proceeds from the sale of the pamphlet to the relief of those imprisoned for debt in London's Newgate Prison.

### III  *Attack on George Washington*

During his ten-month imprisonment, Paine had become increasingly distressed and then angered by the failure of the American government to intercede on his behalf. His many letters to Washington went unanswered, and his claim of American citizenship brought no response from the French. Some evidence exists that the American minister to Paris, Gouverneur Morris, conspired to keep Paine in prison while leading him to think that he was working to help him. At any rate, Paine emerged from prison a bitter man, and he penned in 1794 a venomous letter to George Washington in which he vented the hatred he now felt toward his former friend.

The *Letter to Geroge Washington* aroused a storm when it was published; and, along with the hostile reception of *The Age of Reason,* it seriously eroded the respect Paine had previously commanded. The Federalists, who used the letter to their advantage, touted it as proof of the determination of the French revolutionists to overthrow American institutions by using Paine to undermine the popular respect for Washington. Furthermore, they saw Paine's friendship with Monroe as proof that radical forces in America were involved in a gigantic conspiracy.[3]

The Americans, who by and large admired Washington, were understandably incensed by Paine's scathing attack on the President. Paine accused him of using the powers of his office to line his own pockets and those of his friends; for, when he became President, Paine declares, "the chief of the army became the patron of the fraud" (II, 693). Moreover, Paine questioned Washington's military leadership; he accused him of "cold and unmilitary conduct" and of having "slept away your time in the field, till the finances of the country were completely exhausted, and you have but little share in the glory of the final event" (II, 695). Paine terms Washington's neglect of him during his imprisonment as "a cold deliberate crime of the heart" (II, 710): "you folded your arms, forgot your friend and became silent" (II, 707). Washington is, in fact, incapable of friendship, Paine charges. "It has for some time been known by those who know him, that he has no friendships; that he is incapable of forming any; he can serve or desert a man, or a cause, with constitutional indifference" (II, 698).

## IV   *Last Days*

Although Paine wanted to return to America with the Monroes, the risk was too great that the ship would be stopped and searched by the British; for capture and return to England would have meant Paine's immediate execution. By 1802, however, the seas had become safer; and the sixty-five-year-old revolutionary embarked in the fall for America and landed in Baltimore two months later. As he wrote back to his friend Clio Rickman, "You can have no idea of the agitation which my arrival occasioned."[4] He immediately wrote to Jefferson to inform him that he had brought from Europe "several cases of models, wheels, etc" which he hoped to be able to show the President shortly.

Though Jefferson received Paine cordially and had him to the White House on several occasions, the Federalist press, which conducted an unrelenting smear campaign, hoped to discredit Jefferson in the process. Indeed, Paine's return and his obvious friendship with the President gave the hostile Federalists a hitherto unhoped-for opportunity. Because *The Age of Reason* and the attack on Washington had made Paine an unpopular figure in America, he was a prime target for the anti-Jefferson faction. As J. W. Knudson indicates, the Federalist newspapers throughout the country denounced Paine "as irreligious, depraved, unworthy to associate with the President of the United States, the assassin of Washington's character, and a journalistic hack who peddled his wares to the highest bidder."[5]

When Paine returned to New York in 1803, he was repeatedly snubbed. On the way, he had visited his property at Bordentown; and, when he attempted to catch the stage to New York at Trenton, he was refused passage. The driver claimed that he feared God would strike the carriage with a bolt of lightning should he allow such an infidel to ride in his conveyance. Knudson reports that Grant Thorburn, a minister in New York, was dismissed from his pulpit for shaking hands with Paine.[6]

The aging Paine began to experience periodic attacks of bad health, and he suffered in 1806 a slight stroke. Since his mental powers remained undiminished, he began to plan part III of *The*

*Age of Reason;* and, as a preface to his projected work, he finished *An Essay on Dream,* which dealt with the biblical prophecies, in particular those prophecies concerning the coming of Christ.

The final years of Paine's life were spent in New York City. By early 1809 his infirmity had so progressed that he was having to pay twenty dollars a week for care. Though his body grew steadily weaker, his mind remained clear, and he continued to read and to write letters. Knowing the end was near, Paine made his will and asked to be buried in the Quaker cemetery; but, even though Paine offered to pay, the Quaker committee refused his request. When the aged patriot died peacefully on the morning of June 8, 1809, Madame Margaret Bonneville, her son, and a few friends carried the body to the New Rochelle farm for burial.[7] Legend says that Madame Bonneville stood at one end of the grave and her son at the other and proclaimed as the first spade of earth fell: "Oh, Mr. Paine, my son stands here as testimony of the gratitude of America, and I for France!"[8]

## CHAPTER 6

# The Reputation of Thomas Paine

## I   1791–1899

INTEREST in Paine did not die when the man died; on the contrary, he became the subject of more controversy after his death than at any time during his life. After he wrote *The Age of Reason,* he was denounced as an infidel, a sot, an adulterer — and these accusations accumulated for generations. Mostly ignored by historians and treated perfunctorily by other than controversial writers, Paine did not elicit any great amount of objective notice until near the end of the nineteenth century.

The first of many biographies of Paine was published in 1791 under the lengthy title *The Life of Thomas Paine, the author of Rights of men. With a defence of his writings. By Francis Oldys, A.M., of the University of Pennsylvania.* It has been theorized, but never proved conclusively, that the elaborate pseudonym was contrived by George Chalmers, a minor official in the British government, who was employed to write a biography that would undermine public confidence in Paine and his writings.[1] With government support and wide distribution, the book went through ten editions by 1793. While the title suggests that the work is to be a "defence" of Paine's work, it is actually a hostile and prejudiced account; it is colored by party malice to such an extent that a later writer referred to it as "one of the most horrible collections of abuse which even that venal day produced."[2]

The next significant biographical account, James Cheetham's *Life of Thomas Paine,* appeared in 1809, the year of its subject's death. A vituperative and libelous account, Cheetham's work has been called "the first muck-raking biography in American literature."[3] A Manchester hatter by trade, Cheetham had immigrated to

America and had become the editor of a newspaper in New York City. At first friendly to Paine, he became his bitter enemy when Paine publicly denounced him for betraying the Jeffersonian party. Determined to strike back at Paine, Cheetham wrote to Joel Barlow, who advised him not to undertake a biography because readers would not be persuaded to view Paine in any other light than a drunkard and a Deist. If such a life were written, Barlow felt, it would only render the truth more obscure for future biographers. Since this effect was exactly what Cheetham desired, he set to work and brought his biography to press shortly before Paine died. The following brief extract from the work represents the malicious nature of the whole:

Paine had no good qualities. Incapable of friendship, he was vain, envious, malignant; in France cowardly, and everywhere tyrannical. In his private dealings he was unjust, never thinking of paying for what he contracted, and always cherishing deadly resentments against those who by law compelled him to do justice. To those who had been kind to him he was more than ungrateful.... He was guilty of the worst species of seduction; the alienation of a wife and children from a husband, and a father. Filthy and drunken, he was a compound of all the vices.[4]

These harsh judgments, born and nurtured though they were in personal enmity, have, to varying degrees, been applied to Paine to the present day. Although Paine immediately instituted legal proceedings against Cheetham for the scandalous charges and insinuations which had been levied against him, death claimed him before the case came to trial.

The next biographer, William Cobbett, interests us because he illustrates so well the fact that, throughout the last decade of the eighteenth century and almost all of the nineteenth century, there was very little balanced criticism of Paine: one was either a violent antagonist or a militant partisan. Cobbett, however, was both. Having come to America in 1792, Cobbett conceived a dislike for Paine because he associated him with the French revolutionary leaders. However, when Paine published *The Decline and Fall of the English System of Finance*, Cobbett was filled with admiration, primarily because Paine's predictions and proposals buttressed so well his own convictions. Convinced that he had wronged Paine, Cobbett in 1818 announced his intention to write another life of Paine and negotiated with Madame Margaret Bonneville, who had also been preparing a biography. For various reasons, the work was never completed; and, when Cobbett died in 1835, it remained an unfinished sketch.

Not until fifty years after Paine's death did any valid evaluation appear in print. In 1859 Sheldon Frederick published in the *Atlantic Monthly* three essays which dealt with Paine's role in the American war, his activities in England, his involvement in the French Revolution, and his last years in America.[5] Not only did Frederick grasp the essential value of Paine's plain and commonsense style but he was also able to delineate objectively the issues of the Federalist and anti-Federalist factions in which Paine became involved when he returned to America.

As the century passed the three-quarter mark, the Darwinian tempest that continued to rage in America raised gales of controversy over the matter of religion. *The Age of Reason* was once more dragged to the forefront — to be praised by the devoted and to be abominated by the devout. Edwin P. Whipple, writing in *American Literature and Other Papers,* castigated Paine as "the arch infidel ... whom our early and later theologians have united in holding up as a monster of iniquity and unbelief."[6] Even James Parton, the biographer of Jefferson, wrote that "I think his judgment must have been impaired before he could have consented to publish so inadequate a performance."[7]

The most vocal champion of Paine, however, was yet to make himself known. Nationally known as an orator, distinguished and successful as a trial lawyer in New York, Robert G. Ingersoll, "the Great Agnostic," became one of Paine's most outspoken defenders. An avowed enemy of the Christian church, Ingersoll in 1874 lectured on *The Age of Reason;*[8] and he claimed that it had done more to undermine the power of the Protestant church than all other books then known: it "took power from the pulpit and divided it among the pews."[9] In 1877, Ingersoll, waging a running battle with a New York newspaper over the matter of Paine's last days, offered to pay a thousand dollars to anyone who could prove that Paine had died in agony and fear, and that he had been frightened by the clanking chains of devils — the view commonly put forth by religious tracts of the day.[10] The newspaper then published a mass of personal testimony about the dissolute life and character of Paine, and some statements even equated his services during the Revolution with those of Benedict Arnold. Much of this "personal testimony" has subsequently been proved to be fraudulent or is, at best, highly suspect.

While the last two decades of the nineteenth century continued to bring forth both partisan and unfavorable estimations of Paine, the more influential journals and critical writers were slowly revising the traditional notions and were approaching Paine with a more unbiased attitude. Too, the final decade of the century was to see the publication of the most scholarly work on Paine to date, Moncure Conway's *The Life of Thomas Paine.*

Whereas Sir Leslie Stephen in the first edition of his *History of English Thought in the Eighteenth Century* had made numerous disparaging remarks about Paine, he publicly admitted his ignorance when Conway later pointed out his errors.[11] Furhtermore, he altered the statements in the second edition of the work (1881) and later wrote for the *Dictionary of National Biography* what perhaps is the best short account available of Paine's life.

Not all critics were so magnanimous, of course, C. F. Richardson in 1887 wrote that "[*The Age of Reason*] is popular only with the lower classes, unable to perceive its cheap and unscholarly critical method and its vulgar temper."[12] Perhaps the most famous disparagement, however, was that made by Theodore Roosevelt in his biography of Gouverneur Morris.[13] Because it was a judgment passed by such an eminent person, the phrase "filthy little atheist" attached itself so firmly to Paine that it has not been completely dislodged to this day.

In spite of the hostile notices, three publications in particular indicate the growing amount of reputable scholarship which served to reduce the educated ignorance concerning Paine, to remove the tar and feathers which had so long been accumulating. First, there is the valuable 1880 essay on Paine's role in the French Revolution by E. B. Washburne, a former American Minister to France.[14] A sensible and unbiased evaluation, it set aside at the outset the controversy over Paine's religious beliefs and personal habits and reviewed his involvement in French affairs from the early days of the revolution until his release from prison in 1794. Second, there is Moncure D. Conway's *The Life of Thomas Paine* (1892), the most thoroughly researched and documented biography of Paine to appear in the nineteenth century. Although Conway has been criticized for being overly sympathetic to his subject, most critics concede that he proved conclusively that Paine has been greatly misunderstood and that his services to this country have been understated.

Third, there is M. C. Tyler's *The Literary History of the American Revolution.* While he restricted his survey to the period of the Revolution, Tyler regarded Paine's services as invaluable and termed him "a leader born to lead," as a leader with "language, which at times, was articulate thunder and lightning."[15] Reading Tyler leaves us with the impression that the ultimate success of the patriots during those trying times was due in no small measure to the unflagging and unselfish efforts of the author of *Common Sense* and *The Crisis,* documents which had been pushed out of the public consciousness in the nineteenth-century turmoil over the controversial *Age of Reason.*

## II   *Paine and Progressivism: 1900–20*

The first two decades of the twentieth century constituted an era of striking social and material achievement, an energetic era in which every index promised continued growth and prosperity. The liberal sentiment which dominated the period and manifested itself in the bipartisan reform crusade known as Progressivism was a clearly discernible influence on Paine's reputation. But, though Paine gained in respectability as the century unfolded, he was still subject during this period to hostile attacks from the Catholic press, from those persons holding strictly orthodox religious views, and from those journals controlled or influenced by persons antagonistic toward Paine.

An example of the treatment Paine received at the hands of the Catholic press can be seen in a 1914 issue of the *American Catholic Quarterly Review.*[16] With the stated purpose of counteracting the "many favorable mentions of Paine that have lately been appearing," the anonymous writer tagged Paine "the English infidel writer" in the opening sentence. More than half of the article was made up of a letter which purportedly detailed a visit made by two priests to Paine during his final illness. Written more than thirty years after Paine's death, the letter recalled in detail every sentence uttered and went to great length to depict Paine as "a monster . . . a wretched being . . . besmeared with filth. . . ."[17]

Similarly, when E. C. Moses proposed in *Americana* to arrive at a "fair estimate of the real Thomas Paine,"[18] he concluded that no valid or extenuating excuse "ever has been found to justify Paine's labored attacks on the Bible." Furthermore, in attempting to prove that these writings were demoralizing to the religious beliefs of the people of that time, Moses stated that Paine "once submitted some of his writings which antagonized religion to Mr. Franklin, and the sage displayed much wisdom and tolerance in his kindly advice to the writer." [19] Although Moses quoted in full this particular letter in which Franklin advised against publication of the manuscript, no proof exists that it was Paine to whom Franklin was writing, nor is there any evidence that Paine ever sent to Franklin for his consideration any of his religious writings in their manuscript form.

When the hundredth anniversary of Paine's death was commemorated in 1909, the *Outlook,* a journal heavily influenced by Theodore Roosevelt (who was, in fact, a contributing editor), set forth reasons why it was unable to join in the commemoration. While several other widely read journals carried articles favorable to Paine,[20] the *Outlook* derided him as an author who "made no attempts to understand either the Bible or the reasons why it had for ages been regarded with veneration." In response to many letters which protested the position of the journal, *Outlook* renewed the attack by censuring Paine for his "audacity of ignorance" in writing *The Age of Reason* without having before him a copy of the Bible for reference.[21]

There was also produced during this period quite a large body of work characterized by its enthusiastic — but uncritical — acclaim of Paine. Such vocal champions as W. M. Van der Weyde, J. E. Remsburg, and Elbert Hubbard published much of this material through the auspices of the Thomas Paine National Historical Association, which had been organized in 1906. A typical example of this extremely adulatory writing is that produced by Remsburg, a well-known writer and lecturer on behalf of freethought and state secularization. Remsburg claimed that Paine, Jefferson, Washington, Franklin, Lincoln, and U.S. Grant all were united in a common bond — disbelief in Christianity.[22]

In a similar uncritical vein, Marilla Ricker heaped effusive praise on Paine,[23] while the popular poetess Ella Wheeler Wilcox offered saccharine testimonies. In a sweeping generalization, she claimed that we owe our independence to Paine's writings, that *The Crisis* alone saved the cause from dissolution, that Paine was the prime mover in the establishment of the American republic.[24] Elbert

Hubbard, too, offered regular cloying tributes; for, in his pamphlet entitled *Thomas Paine,* he lapsed regularly into ecstatic praise. He regarded Paine as the savior of the world; compared him to other such saviors as Socrates, Jesus, and Galileo; and gave to him a "supernal position in the galleries of fame."[25]

Although the production of effusive tributes continued throughout the period, a significant number of critical appraisals were written. I. W. Riley, a Johns Hopkins Research Scholar, published a carefully documented study of the early schools of American philosophy in which he dealt with Paine in relation to the Deistic movement.[26] C. E. Persinger's essay on Paine's political philosophy[27] and J. A. Roberts's address to the New York State Historical Association[28] show an increasing tendency to discuss the religious writings in terms of eighteenth-century Deism rather than as offensive, heretical works and to analyze the political writings in terms of their stylistic qualities.

A sampling of the works produced by historians and political scientists shows that Paine, although occasionally neglected, generally was accorded more favorable attention than he had received from the literary historians. Woodrow Wilson, at that time president of Princeton University, did not view Paine as one of the founders of the republic in his impressive *History of the American People* (1902), but he did stress the importance of *Common Sense* as a pamphlet which "thrust constitutional argument upon one side and spoke flatly for independence."[29] Noted as a skillful and effective speaker himself, Wilson emphasized Paine's absolute mastery of the techniques of persuasive writing.

Because of Paine's qualities as a propagandist, there has tended to be a resurgence of interest in him during periods of national stress. Therefore, when America turned full attention to winning World War I, the Committee on Public Information, that arm of the government responsible for molding public opinion, discovered in Paine's writing a rich source of material for its propaganda literature. The promoters of the Liberty Loan emblazoned their posters with quotations from *The Crisis,* and the *New York Times* called attention to the fact that "there was a long time — and it was not so very long ago — when the name of THOMAS PAINE was anathema with many a good pious soul. Today, with the entrance of the United States into the war, the words and teachings of this great writer of the days of the American Revolution are being brought vividly home to us...."[30] Finally, tangible evidence of the spreading liberal attitude in America was the placing of Paine's bust in Independence Hall in 1905 and his nomination to the Hall of Fame in 1920.

### III   *Paine in the Dollar Decade: 1921-29*

Paine's position as an increasingly respectable figure in literature is shown by the several editions of his writings which appeared during this period. In 1922 Carl Van Doren, a name which yet ranks high in American scholarship, edited a volume of Paine selections for the Modern Library. He presented Paine as "the Ragged Philosopher of his race ... [who] like a different Socrates ... brought philosophy to the people."[31] Moreover, a ten-volume Patriot's Edition of Paine's writings appeared in 1925 under the editorship of W. M. Van der Weyde. The first volume, a biography, opened with an introduction by Thomas A. Edison, long a vocal admirer of Paine, who noted that a separate chapter had been devoted to Paine's inventions, an area in his career that most literary critics tended to overlook.[32]

The third, and more important edition of Paine, however, was A. W. Peach's *Selections from the Works of Thomas Paine* (1928).[33] In a lengthy introduction, Peach offered an essentially biographical account of Paine's career, some valuable comments about his method and style, and a concluding estimate of Paine's significance. In spite of Howard Mumford Jones's criticism that Peach had failed to focus his material from the point of view of Paine as an eighteenth-century English writer,[34] Peach's comments on the quality of Paine's mind, his assessment of the basic strengths and weaknesses of *Common Sense,* and his analysis of Paine's method and style were both valid and informative.

In addition to Van der Weyde's *Life,* two biographies were published in the 1921–29 period. F. J. Gould's *Thomas Paine,* [35] one of the popular Roadmaker Series, appeared in 1925, and Mary A. Best's *Thomas Paine: Prophet and Martyr of Democracy,* in 1927.[36] Notably free of the adulatory overtones present in so much of the writing about Paine, Gould's book attempted to establish Paine in an historical perspective by noting social and economic happenings of the time and by accounting for Paine's emergence in the disparity which existed in England between economic and social expansion.

Best wrote in the foreword to her book that "Paine translated the most advanced thought of his time into the vernacular,"[37] and it was into the slangy vernacular of the 1920's that she endeavored to translate Paine. In the manner of Lytton Strachey, the well-known popularizer of the lives of great men, Best aimed her work at the man on the street by framing her prose in the slanglike language which she thought he best understood. "Even morons and movie fans can understand it,"[38] one reviewer wrote.

While Paine received more notice in the periodical press than in book-length studies, one such study, Gamaliel Bradford's *Damaged Souls,*[39] which viewed Paine as a rebel who utilized destruction rather than construction as a method of achieving his idealistic goals, elicited a good deal of response from critics who, in varying degrees, refuted, imitated, or elaborated his thesis. The two extremes of adoration and aspersion continued to be seen, and the Catholic press maintained its traditionally negative line.[40] Overall, however, *The Age of Reason* tended to become less of an issue in periodical literature.

The definitive work of the decade — definitive in terms of criticism of American literature — was V. L. Parrington's *Main Currents in American Thought* (1927), which reinterpreted American literature from its beginnings to 1920 in realistic, socio-economic terms and from a liberal agrarian point of view. Parrington's principal treatment of Paine was found in a section labelled "Tom Paine: Republican Pamphleteer." Given Parrington's liberal bias, we can logically assume that he dealt with Paine in a most favorable fashion, and, in fact, his treatment was in large measure responsible for the sympathetic appraisals which appeared in the 1930's.

Having termed Paine "the first modern internationalist," Parrington saw him as the victim of an *"odium theologicum et politicum,* without parallel in our history," but he noted that "the years are bringing a larger measure of justice to him." The essential value of Parrington's estimate, however, is his analysis of the political theory underlying Paine's principal polemical pieces. He concluded that *Common Sense* was "a notable contribution to the new philosophy of republicanism," that *Rights of Man* was "the most influential English contribution to the revolutionary movement," and that *Agrarian Justice* was "the ripest product of Paine's speculations about the relationship of the government to the individual."[41]

As the decade neared its close, the appearance of several notable works of history and political science insured that Paine, both as a literary and an historical figure, would command more respectful treatment in 1930 than he had in 1920. Gilbert Chinard in his 1929 work on Jefferson called attention to the similarity of the views of Jefferson and Paine, and he admitted that in an earlier work he had mistakenly attributed to Jefferson a document written by Paine.[42] S. E. Morison, one of America's most respected historians, in the same year termed *Common Sense* "the first important republican tract to be issued in America, the first to turn colonial resentment against George III, and the first to present cogent arguments for independence."[43]

In *A History of Political Theories from Rousseau to Spencer* (1926), perhaps the most significant work of political science written during the era, W. A. Dunning viewed Paine as "primarily and essentially an agitator and a pamphleteer rather than a detached and systematic philosopher; but he had a wonderful faculty of both thought and expression, and his keen wit and vivid phrases caught and fixed the doctrine of the revolution often much more effectively than the weightier and deeper analysis of mightier intellects."[44] Dunning showed none of the prejudices attributable to the traditional hostility of the orthodox; rather, he examined Paine solely on the basis of his contribution to the field of political theory.

## IV  *A New Deal for Paine: 1930–41*

The general stirring of interest in American literature which took place in the 1920's developed during the 1930's into a movement whose critical impulse triggered the production of an unceasing stream of books and articles that explored almost every conceivable aspect of our literature. The Depression years, though barren in many respects, were, as far as our national literature is concerned, a bountiful time indeed. And Paine, like so many other figures of the early period, was to receive greater attention than had been previously accorded him.

The first edition of Paine's works during this period that included any substantial critical introduction was that of James S. Allen in 1937. Allen's frequent use of the words "bourgeois," "masses," and "manifestoes" indicated that, in some respects, his evaluation was to be as doctrinaire as Paine himself. Strongly Socialist in outlook, Allen wrote of Paine's advocacy of world revolution for the attainment of democracy, of his "bourgeois-democratic internationalism," of his "direct challenge to the basic principles of capitalistic society."[45]

In 1939, when Harry Hayden Clark published *Six New Letters of Thomas Paine,* he set forth in the introduction the unusual view that Paine, contrary to the popular view, was not a "rebel," hostile to all restraint, but had much in common with the conservatives in the period before the French Revolution. To support his thesis, Clark cited as evidence Paine's connection during the early period with such conservative Federalists as Morris and Hamilton, his advocacy of a stronger federal union, his opposition to paper money as a device for cheating creditors, and his agreement with the majority of Federalists on the issues of Christianity and the Bible.[46]

Paine's interest in the underdog, his preoccupation with economic problems, and his active indignation over injustices of any kind found a modern counterpart in John Dos Passos, a popular novelist of the 1930's whose writing has often been viewed as proletarian propaganda. In 1940, Dos Passos selected what he considered to be the essence of Paine's thought from his better-known writings and published it as *The Living Thoughts of Tom Paine.* The lengthy essay which prefaced the selections, while primarily biographical, exhibited Dos Passos's characteristic accuracy of detail by incorporating numerous letters of Paine and his contemporaries. Not only did this material lend an air of authenticity to the essay but also it tended to verify the author's particular picture of Paine. A conscientious craftsman, Dos Passos utilized a six-part structure in the introduction; and these parts, with the exception of the first, corresponded to the broadly discernible periods in Paine's career. The first part, in some respects the most interesting, clearly established Dos Passos's strong Marxist bent: a brief exposition — an harangue almost — about English tyranny during the reign of George III, with a strong emphasis on the absolutist nature of the government, painted in the background colors of the picture in which Paine was to be the dominant figure.[47]

Paine emerges from the pages of this easily comprehended essay as a fearless, courageous man who held strong beliefs and who expressed them in clarion tones for the common people. Paine did not regard the opinions of others or the conditions around him, and he had no thought of the consequences for himself. A man whose temper and train of thought did not always match the popular mind, he was a man, in fact, much like Dos Passos himself.

The 1930–41 period saw the appearance of four biographies of Paine, all of which were aimed at the general reader. The first of these "popular" lives was George Creel's *Tom Paine — Liberty Bell* (1932),[48] a partisan work totally unencumbered by any of the apparatus of scholarship. Creel, as one reviewer noted, was an able propagandist himself; and, had he chosen to do so, he could have offered a valuable study of Paine's pamphlets as specimens of the art of propaganda. Rather, he "expended his talents in propagandizing Paine"[49] by laboring for the well-turned phrase, by spewing forth a steady stream of unremitting adulation.

The two-hundredth anniversary of Paine's birth was commemorated in America in 1937 by the publication of Hesketh Pearson's *Tom Paine: Friend of Mankind.*[50] Seeking to impart something unique to his book, Pearson claimed to write of Paine "primarily as a man, not the founder of a faith or the formulator of a political philosophy . . . [for] human beings are much more interesting than their causes or their beliefs."[51] Like Creel, Pearson attempted to give the lay reader what he considered to be a reasonably true and, at the same time, entertaining narrative. To some extent, Pearson's book was successful: it did offer a fast-paced, lively account of the important episodes in Paine's life, together with the better-known passages from his writings. For the general public, largely unacquainted with Paine, it may have been entirely satisfactory. However, a too-free handling of sources and a strong tendency toward hero-worship made the work of little value to students. As one reviewer succinctly stated, the book "obscures old questions and leads to no fresh horizons."[52]

The most disjointed, partisan, and inept biography to appear in the period, however, was S. M. Berthold's *Thomas Paine: America's First Liberal* (1938).[53] Carrying the reader on a slapdash excursion over the main facts of Paine's life, Berthold's book gave no new information and was colored everywhere by the author's violent prejudices. Undocumented and unbibliographed, the work

shamelessly eulogized Paine as Berthold, with single-minded determination, attempted to secure for his subject the "exalted position
his unique and extraordinary services so richly deserve."[54]

Frank Smith's *Thomas Paine: Liberator* (1938),[55] yet another of
the lives aimed at the popular reader, had much to recommend it: it
was carefully researched, though undocumented; and it made use
of some new material. The prose was clear and readable; the material was well proportioned, forcefully presented, and the narrative
flow sustained at a fairly fast pace; the situational circle at any
given point in the book was widened by the careful establishment of
historical perspective, and Paine, though always at the center of the
circle, did not necessarily dominate it.

On the other hand, the book could be faulted at several points.
First, its partisan nature was patently obvious; Smith, like the previous popularizers, was unable to achieve any pronounced degree
of objectivity toward his subject. Second, his identification with
Paine was so complete that he tended to see events "about as Paine
saw them, as a struggle of peoples against tyrants and selfish factions,"[56] as one reviewer put it. As a result, a simplistic "good guys
vs. bad guys" view gave that section of the book a somewhat grade-
schoolish cast. Third, the lack of documentation, bibliography, or
index invalidated any scholarly application the book might otherwise have had. Yet, in spite of its shortcomings, Smith's biography
stood as the best account of Paine since Conway's study.

Interestingly enough, Paine merited rather close observation in
two categories of books other than biographies in the 1930–41
period: those in the first half of the decade which were concerned
with studying the adjustments made to religion in the eighteenth
century, and those several works of the latter half which traced the
careers of individuals who have made significant contributions to
social, economic, and political change. The first of the books on
the religious adjustment was G. A. Koch's *Republican Religion*
(1933), which was a study of the movement to establish Deism as a
religious cult. Writing of Paine's relationship with the militant
Deist Elihu Palmer, Koch viewed Paine as the next most important
leader, "wholly in sympathy with Palmer's activities in promoting
the religion of Deism in New York."[57]

W. M. Horton's *Theism and the Scientific Spirit* (1933), a work
which dealt with the fundamental problem of belief in God, presented Paine as a typical member "of that small, uncompromising

group called the Deists," and as a man of the Newtonian Age, whose idea of the world as a "machine" and God as a "mechanic" was typical of the time.[58] In the first of several works which traced the careers of individuals who made significant contributions in some specific area of American life or thought, W. P. Rusterholtz presented in *American Heretics and Saints* (1938) what he termed an "historical resumé of the development of liberal and progressive religion in America." Rusterholtz labelled Paine a universalist, the only "inspired and articulate 'universalist' in the scientific, philosophical and religious connotations of the word in his generation."[59]

Father J. H. Fichter's *The Roots of Change* (1939) was a work of similar design; however, the author chose to write about not religious liberals, but fourteen outstanding leaders who occupied an important place in the history of the relationship between classes of society. This book was doubly significant because it offered the first appraisal by one of the Catholic priesthood that was not an out-and-out attack on Paine. Like previous Catholic writers, Father Fichter maintained that Paine never understood the doctrines of Christian revelation nor the meanings of Christian tradition, but, he carefully qualified, "he was never an atheist."[60]

Yet another work of this type was H. W. Hintz's *The Quaker Influence in American Literature* (1940). Structuring his book as a series of short studies which suggested the prominence and significance of the Quaker influence in American letters, Hintz noted such evidences in Paine's activities and writings. In the concluding paragraph of his chapter devoted to Paine, Hintz offered a significant estimation of his reputation: "Within recent times, however, as has been suggested, careful historians and liberal critics have increasingly recognized his integrity of mind, his breadth of vision and spirit, and his power of thought and expression. The whole tendency today is to regard him as one of the greatest progressives and liberal influences in the entire history of American thought."[61]

Prior to 1930, there were two generally accepted interpretations of Paine. He was either viewed as an honorable champion of liberty who succumbed in his old age to a deplorable religious infidelity or as an individual whose thought was explicable only by the intensity of his Quakerism. While these interpretations continued to be subscribed to, the increasing interest in American literature in the 1930–41 period resulted in Paine's becoming the subject of more frequent and more scholarly investigation than he had heretofore received.

This increase can be seen as early as 1930, when biographer Frank Smith published new information about Paine's first year in America and also proved conclusively that Paine was not the author of "An Occasional Letter on the Female Sex," an essay long attributed to him.[62] E. N. Hooker, investigating the background of William Wordsworth's "Letter to the Bishop of Llandaff," wrote that Paine, "probably the most widely-read writer of the decade, and certainly the most brilliant journalist," exerted a strong influence on the great Romantic poet.[63]

The publication of three important articles by Harry Hayden Clark not only greatly enhanced the critical reception of Paine but also firmly established Clark as one of the most reliable and perceptive critics of early American literature. Clark interpreted Paine's religion from an historical viewpoint by isolating rationalistic science as expounded by the Newtonians as the understructure of his constructive religious thought; he examined Paine's theories of rhetoric; and he explored the ramifications of scientific and humanitarian Deism in Paine's thinking and writing.[64]

The bicentennial of Paine's birth resulted in much notice in the press. In 1936 the *New York Times* announced that a statue of Paine by the noted sculptor Gutzon Borglum would be unveiled in Paris as "part of a worldwide celebration of the two-hundredth anniversary of the noted patriot and humanitarian." The paper later carried an illustration of the statue, which depicted Paine rising in the National Assembly to plead for the life of Louis XVI.[65] *Unity,* a liberal Midwestern monthly, devoted its entire January issue to Paine,[66] and shortly before the January birthdate the *New York Times* ran a feature article which magnanimously stated that Paine "represents in many ways the highest idealism, the deepest faith in the 18th century, translated brilliantly into journalistic terms and sustained by a character as unselfish as Washington's own."[67] Furthermore, public exhibits of Paineiana were opened at the New York Public Library and in Philadelphia, where Richard Gimbel made available nearly a thousand items from his vast personal collection.

Literary historians and compilers of anthologies followed, for the most part, Bradford's well-blazed trail when they described Paine as one who utilized destructive rather than constructive means to achieve his goals; and many, like Carl Van Doren, modified their earlier estimations to reflect this popular "specialist-in-revolutions" motif. The temper of the 1930's was especially congenial to the thesis that Paine was an idealist who would wreak destruction in order to construct a better society. The old animosity toward *The Age of Reason* was almost entirely absent; in fact, when the work was mentioned at all, it was in terms of its Deistic concepts.

Like the playwrights and novelists of the period, the professional historians wrote from a more socially conscious point of view than they had in the preceding decade. Noticeable, too, especially as concerns Paine's reputation, is the influence of the vocal Marxist minority whose assumptions about the nature of society provided a strong impulse for intellectual expression in the 1930's. The tendency to view Paine as a "mania-driven revolutionary" or as a "fiery-eyed radical" diminished, however, as the decade drew toward a close. In fine, Howard Hintz succinctly captured the prevailing wind of opinion concerning Paine in the 1930's when he penned the following sentence: "The whole tendency today is to regard him as one of the greatest progressives and liberal influences in the entire history of American thought."[68]

## V Paine in Conflict, Confrontation, and Crisis: 1942-70

Generally regarded as an age of prosperity and affluence, the 1942-70 era saw not only tremendous scientific and technological advancement but also war and strife. While it was an age which saw a reaffirmation of fundamental civil — Paine would have called them "natural" — rights of citizens, it was also an era in which a militant radical Right sought to suppress divergence of opinion. However, in spite of the recurring crises, the period saw the production in America of more books and articles about Paine than in all the preceding periods combined.

The two most notable editions of Paine's writing to appear in the period were those of Harry Hayden Clark and Philip S. Foner. Clark's volume of selections offered a closely documented introduction which was, according to its author, devoted entirely "to the development of Paine's ideas — religious, political, economic, humanitarian, educational, and literary — with emphasis on their genetic interrelationships."[69] While much of the introduction represented a synthesis of Clark's previously published writings on Paine, the emergent view of Paine was that of a Deist of the Enlightenment who was conditioned largely by the Newtonian concept of a universe guided by inexorable and divinely created laws. One reviewer termed the work "the best analysis in print of Paine's ideas and sources."[70]

Foner's two-volume edition of Paine's complete writings[71] was attractive to the general reader as well as to the student because of its modernized spelling, capitalization, and punctuation. Its introduction offered a factual, restrained account that was free of exaggerated praise of its subject. Acknowledging at the outset the importance of the studies of Conway and Clark, Foner maintained that both had erred in placing too much emphasis on the influence of Quakerism and Newtonianism, for his own thesis was that "life itself was an extremely important teacher."[72] Furthermore, Foner did not subscribe to the "restless rebel" idea; rather, he saw Paine as a lover of liberty who possessed a unique gift and happened to be in the right place at the right time.

Howard Fast, long associated with left-wing American political groups and one of the pronounced Paine champions of this period, issued in 1945 a one-volume edition whose brief introduction presented Paine as "a revolutionist who created a revolution ... a stiff-necked, defiant prophet ... who stepped off a boat and into the ripest and most gorgeous revolutionary opportunity that had existed."[73] Throughout, Fast stressed Paine's affinity with the common people, the dynamic nature of his work, and his belief in the efficacy of change.

Other significant editions of Paine were those of N. F. Adkins and Sidney Hook. Adkins's substantial introduction had as its purpose, "in part, to trace out in Paine's life and works what he believed the proper functioning of humanitarian principles,"[74] but Hook asserted that Paine's belief in "the traditional doctrines of the existence of a Supreme Power and the immortality of the soul was much more unqualified than the belief of Tillich and Niebuhr, the leading Protestant theologians of the twentieth century."[75] Clearly, the day of abrasive attacks on Paine, attacks motivated by religious antagonisms, was over — at least among the considerable number of Paine editors in the 1942–70 period.

As noted earlier, interest in Paine has always seemed to increase in time of war; and this tendency can clearly be seen in 1943 when bookshop windows began displaying copies of Howard Fast's *Citizen Tom Paine,* a novel which can claim with some justification to be the most well-known work about Paine produced in the twentieth century. The first fictionalized account of Paine, Fast's novel was spirited, swift-paced; its prose clean and sharp; its portrait of Paine vivid, revolting yet compelling. The most important feature of the novel, however, was the depiction of its central character, a view which was to exert a definite influence on subsequent treatments of Paine. The figure which emerged from Fast's facile pen was a surly, hulking, twisted-eyed individual — certainly a striking contrast to the saintly martyr of democracy of the popular biographies. Throughout, Fast presented Paine as mania-driven, a man impelled to incite revolution because he could not look around him and see men everywhere free, a man who perfected the "technique of revolution" in order to bring "the common men of the world marching together, shoulder to shoulder, guns in their hands, love in their hearts."[76]

W. E. Woodward's *Tom Paine: America's Godfather* (1945) appeared as the latest in the lengthening list of popular biographies. After having stated in the preface that it was his purpose to present "a true picture of Tom Paine and his place in American history,"[77] Woodward proceeded to churn out what was essentially a panegyric, a potboiler notable only for its extended defense of Paine against charges of drunkenness and uncleanliness, its copious quotations, its careless scholarship, and its almost total lack of interpretation.

The final biography to be published in the 1900–70 period was A. O. Aldridge's *Man of Reason: The Life of Thomas Paine* (1959). Like Woodward, Professor Aldridge announced at the outset that it was his intention "not to please either Paine's idolators or his enemies, but to gather and present documentary evidence."[78] Unlike Woodward, however, Aldridge carried out this intention; the resultant work was so remarkably objective, in fact, that Paine failed to emerge from the pages as a clear-cut personality. This defect was overshadowed, however, by the book's many positive aspects: its use of the "considerable number of documents unknown to any of Paine's editors or his previous biographers";[79] its utilization of the findings set forth in scholarly articles scattered through various journals of the preceding two decades; its firm basis in original research conducted in France and in England as well as in this country.

Aldridge's final chapter, "Recapitulation," can, to a great extent, be regarded as a succinct statement of Paine's position in American literature at the present time. Opening with the statement that the personal neglect suffered by Paine in his last days seems almost incomprehensible, considering the contributions he made "to the development of the nation and to the clarification on a world scale of the principal issues of religion and politics," Aldridge conceded that many of the charges made by Paine's detractors about his personal life and habits had some validity, that Paine's whole life was "a series of contradictions," that he was "a great humanitarian but also a great egotist." Aldridge also contradicted the myth of Paine's "self-sacrificial" pen, and he declined to subscribe to the once popular "ragged philosopher" thesis. Finally, he concluded that Paine's writings on government, economics, and religion are tied together by a unifying theme — the concept of a parallel between the natural universe and the social system, between laws of science and laws of human relationships, and that Paine struck out independently in extending the idea of first principles to politics and economics.[80]

While numerous writers during the "cold" war of the late 1940's and early 1950's presented Paine as a representative of democracy, some writers, on the other hand, used him to illustrate the dangers of suppression of dissension. For example, G. W. Johnson used Paine to illustrate his thesis that the American society must not use legal or extralegal means to suppress opinion: "The story of the American people's dealings with Thomas Paine is one of the most deplorable revelations of a national weakness."[81] Similarly, Norman Thomas developed the idea that society suppresses its dissenters at its peril. Concluding a readable summary of Paine's career, Thomas wrote that "nothing in Paine's life or character extenuates the vicious abuse heaped upon him by pamphleteers and certain biographers."[82]

The fact that Paine has always elicited a lion's share of favorable attention during time of war points out an essential irony: this man, who abhorred war, is, to a great degree indebted to it for the repute he at the present time enjoys. Numerous examples can be cited of the uses made of his propagandistic writings in the war effort of the 1940's as well as in the accolades accorded him as a person.

Addressing the nation on the progress of the war early in 1942, President Franklin D. Roosevelt concluded his speech with a quotation from *The Crisis*.[83] In 1943, an American air squadron stationed in Britain presented to the people of Thetford a memorial plaque to be affixed to the house where Paine was born[84] And in 1945, as the war neared its end, the city of New Rochelle, in public ceremonies presided over by the mayor, officially "restored" to Paine his citizenship rights.[85] The signal event for Paine's reputation, however, was his election in 1945 to the Hall of Fame. Taking notice of this high honor, F. G. Melcher wrote: "His place among our immortals has long been secure in the opinion of those who have studied the forces which made for liberalism and democracy in the young republic ... [and] it has remained for this period of war and debate of fundamental issues to realize what Paine's great pamphlets did in forming public opinion."[86]

During the postwar years, Paine received little notice; but, as America's involvement in the Korean conflict deepened, a predictable flurry of interest materialized. Statues and busts were unveiled, plaques and tablets dedicated, commemorative dinners and essay contests held, and periodicals reflected him relative to the war situation. The first serious American defeat in the winter of 1950 called forth from the *New Republic* a reprinting of Paine's famous first *Crisis* letter and a comparison of the present situation to those bleak days in 1776.[87] A month later *Collier's* made the same comparison, observing that "his words are as apt today as when they were written," and that Paine, if he were alive, would write the same words.[88]

Often embroiled in controversy while he was alive, Paine in 1955 was again the subject of a local fray which received national attention. When a group of Paine's admirers sought to erect a statue of him in Providence, Rhode Island, the mayor blocked the action "because Paine was and remains so controversial a figure."[89] The Civil Liberties Union promptly dispatched a protest to the mayor and blamed the rejection on the predominately Roman Catholic population of the state.[90] The mayor remained intractable and, in fact, not only rejected a revised offer but also turned down the offer of a site as well.[91] Henry Steele Commager, the noted historian, utilized this local flap in an amusing article which he constructed as a dialogue between Paine and an imaginary chairman of the board who was reviewing Paine's credentials to determine whether or not a statue should be authorized.[92]

While attention such as this one perhaps failed to enhance Paine's reputation among the general public, he was the object of much serious study. Aldridge regularly published perceptive analyses of Paine's writings, and Colonel Richard Gimbel, a well-known collector of Paine memorabilia, also wrote several articles, one of which took as its subject the resurgence of Paine.[93] The Yale Library in 1959 opened an exhibit of items from the Gimbel collection in commemoration of the one hundred and fiftieth anniversary of Paine's death.[94]

During the decade of the 1960's America once more went to war, although so slowly did the Southeast Asia involvement develop that Paine was never trotted out to pump up patriotism as had been the case in past wars. Instead, his admirers concentrated on raising funds for yet another statue to commemorate the two hundred twenty-seventh anniversary of his birth. After much prodding, the United States Post Office finally issued a Paine stamp, and in 1970 the Hall of Fame for Great Americans announced the striking of a medal honoring Paine.[95]

CHAPTER 7

# *Conclusion*

THOMAS Paine's place in American literature and history is secure. Although not ranked with Jefferson, Washington, and Franklin, Paine continues to be regarded as one who made a significant contribution in determining the course of a whole people — the American colonists who pursued a course of independence and who established a republican form of government. Paine's special role in this momentous activity was that of a propagandist — a swayer of public opinion who used his pen with consummate skill to incite decisive action in a generally complacent populace. His instinctive knowledge of what moves men to action has never been displayed more skillfully or more successfully than in the pages of *Common Sense* and in the *Crisis* papers. The ringing sentences which filled the breasts of the rude colonials with a burning desire to be their own masters describe a very important part of our national character. Down through the generations every schoolchild has been taught to revere the sentiments to which Paine so eloquently gave voice, ones which he understood so clearly and felt so deeply.

Though persuasive writing was Paine's forte — and we must acknowledge his mastery of rhetoric — to understand fully the man and his writings, we must still look at areas in which his goals were never reached, his ambitions never realized, and try to understand why he did not always succeed. When Paine returned to England, he hoped to bring about the same kind of revolution which he had helped bring to fruition in America. With the same vigor, he devoted himself to a new task — the composition of *Rights of Man*. Why were the selfsame ideas, so successful in America, doomed to failure in England? The reasons are two-fold: Paine did not understand fully the Lockean basis of the American Revolution, nor did he understand constitutional evolution as Burke perceived it.

Paine was a "man-of-the-moment," and this description explains to a great degree why he was so successful in America: he was in the right place at exactly the right time. However, it also explains why he was not successful in England. The moderate course of change which he advocated in *Prospects on the Rubicon,* written soon after he returned, would seem to suggest that he was again reading the national temper correctly; however, he read Burke's *Reflections* and his reactions were, again, of the moment. Burke had been unfair to the French in many of the things he had said about the revolution across the Channel; and Paine, because of his exaggerated sense of empathy with the French people, overreacted and advocated in *Rights of Man* a sudden and complete break with the past, as had been done in France. He even went so far as to recommend representative republicanism for all of Europe, even though such representation had not yet been effected in France; and he suggested broad outlines for carrying out his proposals.

Similarly, the "man-of-the-moment" motif can be seen to be responsible for his violent attack upon organized religion in *The Age of Reason.* Paine, Robespierre, Diderot, Voltaire — all were sons of the Enlightenment and all shared the influence of Newton and Descartes. But Paine, unlike Voltaire, had little sense of humor; therefore, his reaction to organized religion was so deadly serious that he attacked it violently. Unlike Diderot, Paine felt a deep need for the "watchmaker God," and he felt it imperative that he stem the rising tide of atheism in France. Robespierre, too, shared his fear of atheism; but his methods for containing it were unacceptable to Paine, who possessed an acute appreciation for freedom of the individual.

Though *The Age of Reason* is a principal work in the Paine canon, our final opinion of the man should not rest upon this work. The violent assault on Paine's character which resulted from the writing of this book could have been avoided had Paine been less deadly serious, had he possessed something of Voltaire's élan. Perhaps it is best to view this still-controversial work as a classic example of eighteenth-century Deism which has had a decided influence upon subsequent liberal religious thought.

Following this abortive excursion into religion, Paine returned to his first love — political theory. In his last significant work,

*Agrarian Justice,* Paine filled in and elaborated the broad outlines left incomplete in *Rights of Man.* With specific detail he described how republicanism could be used to aid the child, the poor, the sick, and the aged; and this socioeconomic work is his most far-sighted contribution.

Paine was a man without roots, a man who acted for the moment — the only way he could act. Acutely aware of injustice, Paine identified with the people everywhere he went — not with the privileged few, but with the multitudes, who, like him, found their lives, their liberties, their right to happiness circumscribed by a government insensitive to their needs. Paine was true to himself — it was his nature to react instinctively. Too, he was an individual, an originator of action, who never was swept along by forces he did not understand. Always searching for a home, it seems appropriate that this man who regarded himself as an American has no final resting place. Ten years after his death his bones were dug up, removed to England, and finally lost. Thus Paine, born in England, adopted by America, and given citizenship by France, can rightfully be called a citizen of the world. Moreover, his views have been claimed by people anywhere who desire to form for themselves a government which gives to every individual a just measure of liberty.

# Notes and References

## Chapter One

1. George K. Anderson and William E. Buckler, eds., *The Literature of England,* 5th ed. (Chicago, 1966), I, p. 1603.
2. L(eslie) S(tephen), "Paine, Thomas," *Dictionary of National Biography,* XV, 69. Stephen notes that the church register does not record his baptism.
3. Moncure Daniel Conway, *Life of Thomas Paine, 3rd ed. (1892; rpt. New York, 1970). Hereafter referred to as Conway, Life.*
4. R. R. Palmer, "Tom Paine: Victim of the Rights of Man," *Pennsylvania Magazine of History and Biography,* LXVI (April 1942), p. 164.
5. *The Complete Writings of Thomas Paine,* ed. Philip S. Foner (1945; rpt. New York, 1969), I, p. 496. All quotations from Paine's writings, unless otherwise noted, are from this edition.
6. *Ibid.*
7. Alfred Owen Aldridge, "Thomas Paine and the Classics," *Eighteenth-Century Studies,* I (1968), pp. 379–80.
8. For a full consideration of Paine's literary theories, see Harry Hayden Clark, "Thomas Paine's Theories of Rhetoric," *Transactions of the Wisconsin Academy of Sciences, Arts, and Letters,* XXVIII (1933), pp. 307–39.
9. Ralph C. Roper, "Comments and Criticism," *Scientific Monthly,* LVIII (1944), p. 403.
10. Foner, I, p. 405.
11. *Ibid.,* p. 406.
12. A(gnes) M(ary) C(larke), "Ferguson, James," *Dictionary of National Biography,* VI, p. 1210.
13. Harry Hayden Clark, ed., *Thomas Paine: Representative Selections* (New York, 1944), p. xxxv.
14. Clark's Introduction to *Representative Selections* posits the thesis that Newtonianism exerted a greater influence upon Paine than did Quakerism. See also Clark's "Toward a Reinterpretation of Thomas Paine," *American Literature,* V (1933–34), pp. 133–45; and "The Influence of Science on American Ideas, from 1775 to 1809," *Transactions of the Wisconsin Academy of Science, Arts, and Letters,* XXXV (1943), pp. 305–49.

15. Conway, *Life,* p. 7.

16. *Ibid.*

17. Quoted in Conway, *Life,* pp. 10–11.

18. *Ibid.*

19. Hesketh Pearson, *Tom Paine: Friend of Mankind* (New York and London, 1937), p. 7.

20. Conway, *Life.*

21. Foner, II, p. 15.

22. *Ibid.,* p. 1129.

23. *Ibid.,* p. 1129n.

24. Conway, *Life,* p. 12.

25. Quoted in Conway, *Life,* p. 13.

26. C(rane) B(rinton), "Paine, Thomas," *Dictionary of American Biography,* VII, p. 159.

27. Alfred Owen Aldridge, *Man of Reason: The Life of Thomas Paine* (Philadelphia and New York, 1959), p. 28. Hereafter referred to as Aldridge, *Man of Reason.*

28. The Writings of Benjamin Franklin, ed. Albert Henry Smyth (1907; rpt. New York, 1970), VI, pp. 248–49.

## *Chapter Two*

1. Thomas A. Bailey, *The American Pageant: A History of the Republic* (Boston, 1956), p. 90.

2. Ralph Waldo Emerson, "Concord Hymn."

3. *The Correspondence of King George the Third from 1760 to December 1783,* ed. Sir John W. Fortescue (London, 1927), III, p. 153.

4. Quoted in Conway's *Life,* p. 23.

5. Foner, II, p. 1131. Page citations to Paine's writings henceforth will be given parenthetically in text.

6. Gorham Munson, *Twelve Decisive Battles of the Mind* (New York, 1942), p. 35.

7. See Frank Smith, "New Light on Thomas Paine's First Year in America," *American Literature,* I (January 1930), pp. 347–71. Smith lists all articles which Paine contributed to the *Pennsylvania Magazine* during 1775.

8. Aldridge, *Man of Reason,* p. 31.

9. Paine was long thought to have written "An Occasional Letter on the Female Sex," an early plea for equal rights for women, which appeared in the *Pennsylvania Magazine* of August 1775. Frank Smith ("The Authorship of 'An Occasional Letter on the Female Sex,'" *American Literature,* II [November 1930], pp. 277–80) has shown that Paine was not the author, that the essay was lifted bodily from the Russell translation of M. A. L. Thomas's *Essai sur le Caractère, les Moeurs, et l'Esprit des*

*Femmes dans les Différens Siècles,* which had come out in Russell's translation in Philadelphia in 1774.

10. David S. Muzzey, "Thomas Paine and American Independence," *American Review* [Bloomington, Ill.], IV (1926), p. 280.

11. Quoted in Will Payne, "Our First Best-Seller," *Saturday Evening Post,* September 18, 1926, p. 68.

12. Nelson F. Adkins, ed., *Common Sense and Other Political Writings,* The American Heritage Series (Indianapolis, 1953), p. xxiii.

13. Frederick Sheldon, "Tom Paine's First Appearance in America," *Atlantic Monthly,* IV (November 1859), rpt. in Edwin H. Ford and Edwin Emery, eds., *Highlights in the History of the American Press* (Minneapolis, 1954), p. 103.

14. Quoted in Conway's *Life,* p. 27.

15. *The Writings of George Washington,* ed. John C. Fitzpatrick (Washington: United States Printing Office, 1951), IV, p. 297.

16. Quoted in Moses Coit Tyler, *The Literary History of the Revolution,* 2nd ed. (New York, 1898), I, p. 473.

17. *Ibid.*

18. *Ibid.,* p. 474.

19. Vernon L. Parrington, *Main Currents in American Thought* (New York, 1927), I, p. 330.

20. Arthur Wallace Peach, ed., *Selections from the Works of Thomas Paine* (New York, 1928), p. xix.

21. Carl Becker, *The Declaration of Independence* (New York, 1942), p. 24. Becker's second chapter offers one of the most concise yet penetrating discussions of the natural rights philosophy available.

22. Adkins, p. xv.

23. Becker, p. 79.

24. Carl Van Doren, ed., *Selections from the Writings of Thomas Paine* (New York, 1922), p. ix.

25. Edward P. J. Corbett, *Classical Rhetoric for the Modern Student* (New York, 1965), p. 22.

26. Conway, *Life,* p. 26.

27. Henry Leffman, "The Real Thomas Paine, Patriot and Publicist. A Philosopher Misunderstood," *Pennsylvania Magazine of History and Biography,* XLVI (1922), p. 86.

28. Tyler, I, p. 462.

29. Corbett, p. 39.

30. Peach, p. xx.

31. Tyler, I, 468.

32. F. J. McConnell, *Evangelicals, Revolutionists and Idealists: Six English Contributors to American Thought and Action* (New York, 1942), p. 105.

33. Tyler, I, p. 461.

34. Aldridge, *Man of Reason,* p. 43.

35. Thomas R. Adams, "The Authorship and Printing of Plain Truth by 'Candidus,'" *Papers of the Bibliographical Society of America,* 49 (1955), p. 230.

36. Tyler, II, p. 37.

37. George Creel, "Tom Paine, Champion of Liberty," *Mentor* (September 1930), p. 12.

38. *Writings of George Washington,* VI, p. 347.

39. Peach, p. xx.

40. Creel, p. 12.

41. Peach, p. xxii.

42. *Ibid.,* pp. xxiii-iv.

43. *Ibid.,* p. xxiv.

44. *Writings of George Washington,* XVIII, p. 434.

45. Peach, p. xxvii.

46. Tyler, II, p. 42.

47. Van Doren, p. xi.

48. *Ibid.,* p. x.

49. Peach, pp. xxviii-ix.

50. Aldridge, *Man of Reason,* p. 84.

51. *Ibid.,* p. 97.

52. Darrel Abel, "The Significance of the Letter to the Abbé Raynal in the Progress of Thomas Paine's Thought," *Pennsylvania Magazine of History and Biography,* XLVI (April 1942), pp. 177, 181.

53. Aldridge, *Man of Reason,* p. 99.

54. See Harry Hayden Clark, ed., *Six New Letters of Thomas Paine* (Madison, Wisconsin, 1939), pp. i-xxxii. Clark sets forth the view that Paine's work during this period had considerably more in common with those who were later regarded as conservative than has generally been supposed, and that he agreed with the majority of Fedralists on many issues.

55. See Freeman H. Hart, *The Valley of Virginia in the American Revolution* (Chapel Hill, North Carolina, 1942), pp. 128-30. Hart shows that many of the back-country farmers supported Paine's position. For a history of the entire issue, see Janet Wilson, "The Bank of North America and Pennsylvania Politics," *Pennsylvania Magazine of History and Biography,* XLVI (January 1942), pp. 3-28.

56. Foner, II, p. 367.

57. Adkins, p. xxxi.

## Chapter Three

1. Quoted in Conway's *Life,* p. 81.

2. Robert B. Dishman, *Burke and Paine: On Revolution and the Rights of Man* (New York, 1971), p. 52.

3. Aldridge, *Man of Reason,* p. 121.

4. *Ibid.*

5. Audrey Williamson, *Thomas Paine: His Life, Work, and Times* (London, 1973), p. 116.

6. R. R. Fennessy, *Burke, Paine and the Rights of Man* (The Hague, 1963), p. 44.

7. Quoted in Dishman, p. 61.

8. Dishman, p. 65.

9. Fennessy, p. 44.

10. *Burke's Politics: Selected Writings and Speeches,* ed. Ross J. S. Hoffman and Paul Levack (New York, 1967), p. 69.

11. Dishman, pp. 22–25.

12. *Ibid.,* pp. 79, 284 n. 8.

13. *Ibid.,* pp. 81–82, 285 n. 10.

14. *Ibid.,* p. 83.

15. Edmund Burke, *Reflections on the Revolution in France,* ed. Thomas H. D. Mahoney (Indianapolis, Indiana, 1955), pp. 85–86.

16. *Ibid.,* p. 82.

17. *Ibid.,* p. 67.

18. Samuel Edwards, *Rebel: A Biography of Tom Paine* (New York, 1974), p. 121.

19. *Ibid.,* p. 126.

20. Nat Schmulowitz, "Thou Shalt Not Read the Rights of Man," *United States Law Review,* LXXIII (1939), pp. 271–86.

21. Jean Jacques Rousseau, *The Social Contract* in *The Portable Age of Reason,* ed. Crane Brinton (New York, 1967), p. 163.

22. Dishman, p. 112.

## Chapter Four

1. Aldridge, *Man of Reason,* p. 191.

2. "In the beginning was the word [logos] and the word [logos] was with God and the word [logos] was God." — John 1:1. Following this view, the Bible is more accurately thought "to tell of" than "to be" the word of God. Although this view was extremely radical in the eighteenth century, Paine makes it the thesis of his entire treatment of the Old and the New Testaments.

3. Paine claims he could not procure a Bible while writing Part I (I, 514). Although he completed it before he went to prison in December, the French government during the fall of 1793 sought by the most extreme means to stamp out Catholicism. This perhaps explains why Paine was unable to acquire a Bible.

4. When Paine refers to "the immaculate conception," he means the virgin birth of Jesus. It was not until the last half of the nineteenth century that Pope Pius IX proclaimed the doctrine of the Immaculate Conception, the conception of the Virgin Mary in the womb of Saint Anne.

5. Paine refers to the Old Testament as the Bible.

## Chapter Five

1. Foner, II, p. 607 n. 2.

2. Edwards, p. 208.

3. Foner draws these conclusions in his introduction to the *Letter to George Washington,* II, p. 690.

4. Conway, *Life,* p. 279.

5. For a complete account of Paine's reception in America, see Jerry W. Knudson "The Rage Around Tom Paine: Newspaper Reactions to His Homecoming in 1802," *New York Historical Society Quarterly Bulletin,* LIII (1969), pp. 34–63.

6. *Ibid.,* p. 60.

7. Margaret Bonneville was the wife of Nocholas de Bonneville, editor of *Bien Informé,* a paper for which Paine had frequently written during his years in France. When Madame Bonneville and her sons came to America, she earned her living for a time as Paine's housekeeper.

8. Conway, *Life,* p. 323.

## Chapter Six

1. In his biographical sketch of Paine in the *Dictionary of National Biography,* 1921 ed., Sir Leslie Stephen takes important notice of this and cites W.T. Sherwin as the original source of this information.

2. Conway (*Life,* p. xiii) attributes this statement to William Cobbett's biographer, Edward Smith.

3. Aldridge, *Man of Reason,* p. 10.

4. James Cheetham, *The Life of Thomas Paine* (New York, 1809), p. 313.

5. Sheldon Frederick, "Thomas Paine's Second Appearance in the United States, *Atlantic Monthly,* IV (July 1859), pp. 1–17; "Tom Paine's First Appearance in America," IV (November 1859), pp. 565–75; "Thomas Paine in England and in France," IV (December 1859), pp. 690–709.

6. Quoted in the *Library of Literary Criticism of English and American Authors,* ed. C. W. Moulton (Buffalo, New York, 1901–1905), IV, p. 532.

7. James Parton, *Life of Thomas Jefferson* (Boston, 1874), pp. 591–92.

8. This lecture appeared first in Ingersoll's *The Gods and Other Lectures* (New York, 1874), and is reprinted in *Ingersoll's Greatest Lectures* (New York, 1944), pp. 121–65.

9. *Ingersoll's Greatest Lectures,* p. 153.

10. Ingersoll's editorial letters and much of the newspaper's material are cited in *The Works of Robert G. Ingersoll* (New York, 1909), V, pp. 447–524.

11. Sir Leslie Stephen, *History of English Thought in the Eighteenth Century,* 3rd ed., 2 vols. (London, 1927), I, pp. 458–64; II, pp. 260–64. This is a reprint of the 1902 edition, in which Stephen stated in a footnote that he had been wrong in some assertions made in the 1876 edition and had revised his opinions of Paine since reading Conway.

12. Charles F. Richardson, *American Literature, 1607–1885* (New York, 1887), I, p. 211.

13. Theodore Roosevelt, *Gouverneur Morris* (Boston, 1891).

14. E. B. Washburne, "Thomas Paine and the French Revolution," *Scribner's Monthly,* (September 1880), pp. 771–86.

15. Moses Coit Tyler, *The Literary History of the American Revolution, 1763-1783* (New York, 1898), II, p. 42.

16. Anonymous, "Influence of Paine on American Thought: His Sad End," *American Catholic Quarterly Review,* XXXIX (1914), pp. 347–48.

17. *Ibid.,* pp. 349, 352, 355.

18. Ernest C. Moses, "Was Thomas Paine Infidel at Heart," *Americana,* VII (1912), p. 641.

19. *Ibid.,* p. 646.

20. Henry Paradyne, "A Misunderstood Patriot," *Harper's Weekly,* V (June 1909), p. 15; *Current Literature* ("Conflicting Estimates of Thomas Paine," XLVII (1909), pp. 535–36 noted that the greater part of the commentary elicited by the Paine centenary was laudatory, and that indications were that Paine's reputation and influence were steadily improving.

21. Anonymous, "Thomas Paine," *The Outlook,* XCIV (1910), pp. 334–35, 608.

22. J. E. Remsburg, *Six Historic Americans* (New York: Truth Seeker Co., [1906]), p. vii.

23. Ricker's essay "A Square Deal" is found in vol. 1 of *Life and Writings of Thomas Paine,* ed. and annotated by Daniel Edwin Wheeler, 10 vols. (New York, 1908).

24. Ella Wheeler Wilcox, *Lest We Forget* (East Aurora, New York, [1915]), pp. 4–8.

25. Elbert Hubbard, *Thomas Paine* (East Aurora, New York, [1915]), p. 18.

26. I. W. Riley, *American Philosophy: The Early Schools* (New York, 1907), pp. 296–304.

27. Clark Edmund Persinger, "The Political Philosophy of Thomas

Paine," University of Nebraska *Graduate Bulletin,* 7th Series (July 1901), pp. 54-75.

28. J. A. Roberts, "Thomas Paine," *New York State Historical Association Quarterly Journal* I (1920), pp. 73-85.

29. Woodrow Wilson, *A History of the American People,* 5 vols. (New York and London, 1902), III, p. 91.

30. Anonymous, "Editorial," *New York Times,* June 9, 1918, VI, p. 270, col. 2.

31. Carl Van Doren, *Selections from the Writings of Thomas Paine* (New York, 1922), p. vii.

32. W. M. Van Der Weyde, *The Life and Works of Thomas Paine,* Patriot's Edition, 10 vols. (New Rochelle, New York, 1925), I, pp. 1-2.

33. Arthur Wallace Peach, *Selections from the Works of Thomas Paine* (New York, 1928), p. xlvi.

34. Howard Mumford Jones, review of *Selections from the Works of Thomas Paine* by A. W. Peach, *American Literature,* I (1929), pp. 105-106.

35. Frederick J. Gould, *Thomas Paine* (Boston, 1925).

36. Mary A. Best, *Thomas Paine: Prophet and Martyr of Democracy* (New York, 1927).

37. *Ibid.,* p. vii.

38. Charles Lee Snider, "Major Prophet of Democracy," *New York Herald Tribune Books,* June 12, 1927, p. 5.

39. Gamaliel Bradford, *Damaged Souls* (Boston and New York, 1922), pp. 51-84.

40. For examples of the two extreme views of Paine, see J. V. Nash, "An Undamaged Soul: Thomas Paine," *Open Court,* XXXVIII (1924), pp. 577-94; and J. M. Gillis, "Tom Paine," *Catholic World,* CXXI (1925), pp. 48-58.

41. Vernon Louis Parrington, *Main Currents in American Thought,* 3 vols. in 1 (New York, 1927), I, pp. 327, 334, 337.

42. Gilbert Chinard, *Thomas Jefferson: The Apostle of Americanism,* 2nd ed. rev. (1929; rpt. Ann Arbor, Mich., 1957), pp. 82, 227-28, 258-61, 390-91.

43. Samuel Eliot Morison, ed. *Sources and Documents Illustrating The American Revolution 1764-1788 and the Formation of the Federal Constitution,* 2nd ed. (1929; rpt. Galaxy Books, 1965), pp. xxxvi-vii.

44. William Archibald Dunning, *A History of Political Theories from Rousseau to Spencer* (New York, 1926), pp. 110-16.

45. James S. Allen, *Thomas Paine: Selections from His Writings* (New York, 1937), pp. 1-24.

46. Harry Hayden Clark, *Six New Letters of Thomas Paine* (Madison, Wisconsin, 1939), pp. 1-32.

47. John Dos Passos, *The Living Thoughts of Tom Paine* (1940; rpt. New York, n.d.), pp. 7–51.

48. George Creel, *Tom Paine — Liberty Bell* (Boston, 1932).

49. Robert W. Bolwell, *American Literature,* V (1933–34), pp. 284–85.

50. Hesketh Pearson, *Tom Paine: Friend of Mankind* (New York and London, 1937).

51. *Ibid.,* p. ix.

52. Frank Smith, *American Literature,* IX (1937–38), p. 261.

53. S. M. Berthold, *Thomas Paine: America's First Liberal* (Boston, 1938).

54. *Ibid.,* p. 10.

55. Frank Smith, *Thomas Paine: Liberator* (New York, 1938).

56. R. R. Palmer, *Nation,* XCLVII (1938), p. 459.

57. G. Adolph Koch, *Republican Religion: The American Revolution and the Cult of Reason* (1933; rpt. Gloucester, Mass., 1964), p. 130.

58. Walter Marshall Horton, *Theism and the Scientific Spirit* (New York and London, 1933), pp. 51, 52–53, 56.

59. Wallace P. Rusterholtz, *American Heretics and Saints* (Boston, 1938) pp. 107–44.

60. Joseph H. Fichter, S.J., *Roots of Change* (New York, 1939), pp. 65–86.

61. Howard W. Hintz, *The Quaker Influence in American Literature* 1940; rpt. Port Washington, New York, 1965), pp. 17–25.

62. Frank Smith, "New Light on Thomas Paine's First Year in America," *American Literature,* I (1929–30), pp. 347–71; "The Authorship of 'An Occasional Letter on the Female Sex,'" *American Literature,* II (1930–31), pp. 277–80.

63. Edward Niles Hooker, "Wordsworth's Letter to the Bishop of Llandaff," *Studies in Philology,* XXVIII (1931), pp. 522–31.

64. Harry Hayden Clark, "An Historical Interpretation of Thomas Paine's Religion," *University of California Chronicle,* XXXV (1933), pp. 56–87; "Thomas Paine's Theories of Rhetoric," *Trans. Wisconsin Academy of Sciences, Arts, and Letters,* XXVIII (1933), pp. 307–39; "Toward a Reinterpretation of Thomas Paine," *American Literature,* V (1933–34), pp. 133–45.

65. Anonymous, "Paine Statue Planned," *New York Times,* May 22, 1936, p. 21, col. 4; Dec. 27, 1936, sec. 2, p. 3, col. 2.

66. John Haynes Holmes, "Thomas Paine: 1737–1937," *Unity,* CXVIII (1937), pp. 186–89; E. Burdette Backus, "Thomas Paine and the Rights of Man," pp. 190–91; Charles H. Lyttle, "Thomas Paine's Religion of Humanity," pp. 192–93; Curtis W. Reese, "Thomas Paine: A Tribute," pp. 193–94; David Gittleman, "Thomas Paine: American Patriot and Crusader," pp. 194–96.

160 THOMAS PAINE

67. Anonymous, "The Firebrand of the Revolution," *New York Times,* January 24, 1937, sec. 8, p. 10, col. 1.

68. Hintz, p. 24.

69. Harry Hayden Clark, *Thomas Paine: Representative Selections* (New York, 1944), p. v.

70. Philip Davidson, *American Historical Review,* L (1944), pp. 143–44.

71. Philip S. Foner, ed., *The Complete Writings of Thomas Paine,* 2 vols. (1945; rpt. New York, 1969).

72. *Ibid.,* I, p. x.

73. Howard Fast, ed. *The Selected Work of Tom Paine* (New York, 1945), pp. ix, xii.

74. Adkins, pp. l-lii.

75. Sidney Hook, ed., *The Essential Thomas Paine* (New York, 1969), p. xi, xii.

76. Howard Fast, *Citizen Tom Paine* (New York, 1943), p. 124.

77. W. E. Woodward, *Tom Paine: America's Godfather* (New York, 1945), pp. 29–30.

78. Aldridge, *Man of Reason,* p. 9. See Bibliography for biographies of Paine published since 1970.

79. *Ibid.*

80. *Ibid.,* pp. 317–22.

81. Gerald White Johnson, *The Lunatic Fringe* (Philadelphia, 1957), pp. 21–32.

82. Norman Thomas, *Great Dissenters* (New York, 1961), pp. 93–128.

83. Anonymous, "Pres. Roosevelt's Address to Nation on America's Progress in the War," *New York Times,* Feb. 24, 1942, p. 4, col. 7.

84. Anonymous, "Plaque to Thomas Paine Is Unveiled in Britain," *New York Times,* Oct. 22, 1943, p. 4, col. 6.

85. Anonymous, "Paine, Barred from Voting 139 Years Ago, Has Citizenship Restored by New Rochelle," *New York Times,* July 5, 1945, p. 4, col. 3.

86. Frederic G. Melcher, "Authors to the Hall of Fame," *Publisher's Weekly,* CXLVIII (1945), p. 2127.

87. Anonymous, "Say Not That Thousands Are Gone," *New Republic,* December 25, 1950, pp. 13–14.

88. Anonymous, "The Price Is Not Too Great," *Collier's,* January 27, 1951, p. 78.

89. Anonymous, "Thomas Paine Is Still too Controversial, so Providence Doesn't Want Statue of Him, *New York Times,* September 23, 1955, p. 27, col. 6.

90. Anonymous, "Rejection of Tom Paine Statue Inflames Civil Liberties Union," *New York Times,* September 24, 1955, p. 21, col. 4.

91. Anonymous, "Providence Rejects Paine Statue, Park," *New York Times,* October 7, 1955, p. 27, col. 6.

92. Henry Steele Commager, "Tom Paine Talks Back to Providence," *Saturday Review, December 24, 1955, pp. 5-7, 32.*

93. *Colonel Richard Gimbel, "The Resurgence of Thomas Paine," Proceedings of the American Antiquarian Society,* LIX (1959), p. 109.

94. Colonel Gimbel later published the exhibit catalogue as "Thomas Paine Fights for Freedom in Three Worlds: The New, The Old, The Next," *Proceedings of the American Antiquarian Society,* LXX (1960), pp. 397-492.

95. Thomas V. Haney, "American Heritage to be Emphasized," *New York Times,* March 15, 1970, sec. 2, p. 39, col. 2.

# Selected Bibliography

PRIMARY SOURCES

*Common Sense and Other Political Writings*. Ed. Nelson F. Adkins, American Heritage Series. Indianapolis, Ind.: Bobbs-Merrill, 1953. Introduction reviews Paine's career, with special emphasis on the backgrounds of his political speculations. Useful bibliography and explanatory notes.

*The Complete Writings of Thomas Paine*. Ed. Philip S. Foner. Two vols., 1945; rpt. New York: Citadel Press, 1969. Including much new material, this edition utilizes modern spelling, capitalization, and punctuation. Introductory biographical essay presents Paine not as the conventional "restless rebel," but as a world citizen and democrat whose unique pen was moved by events around him. Throughout, the account is restrained, well-researched, and documented. Other features include a chronological table of Paine's writing, a selected bibliography, and substantial editorial notes prefacing each major work. The fullest and most usable edition of Paine yet published.

*Selections from the Works of Thomas Paine*. Ed. Arthur Wallace Peach. New York: Harcourt, 1928. Substantial introduction attempts to assess basic strengths and weaknesses of the more important writings. Summarizes each of the *Crisis* papers and has good comments on Paine's method and style.

*Selections from the Writing of Thomas Paine*. Ed. Carl Van Doren. New York: Boni & Liveright, 1922. Introduction depicts Paine as "the classic textbook of radical thought for the Anglo-Saxon proletariat."

*Thomas Paine: Representative Selections*. Ed. Harry Hayden Clark. American Writers Series, 1944; rpt. New York: Hill and Wang, 1961. Closely documented introduction expands thesis that Newtonianism exerted a greater influence on Paine than did his Quaker background. Notes on selections provide historical criticism, informative background, and succinct analysis. Useful bibliography.

*The Writings of Thomas Paine*. Ed. Moncure D. Conway, 1914; rpt. New York: AMS Press, 1967.

162

SECONDARY SOURCES

1. Biographies

ALDRIDGE, ALFRED OWEN. *Man of Reason: The Life of Thomas Paine.* Philadelphia & New York: Lippincott, 1959. The first twentieth-century biography of Paine to be based on original research in France and England as well as in America. The objective quality, full chapter notes, and scholarly approach make this the best life to date.

CONWAY, MONCURE D. *The Life of Thomas Paine.* 1892; rpt. New York: Benjamin Blom, 1969. Most authoritative work on Paine produced in the nineteenth century; modern critics find too much emphasis placed on the influence of Paine's Quaker upbringing.

EDWARDS, SAMUEL. *Rebel: A Biography of Tom Paine.* New York: Praeger, 1974. Another popular biography; readable but marred by free handling of sources. No documentation.

HAWKE, DAVID FREEMAN. *Paine.* New York: Harper & Row, 1974. Notes, bibliography, illustrations, and readable text are major contributions of this recent life.

PEARSON, HESKETH. *Tom Paine: Friend of Mankind.* New York and London: Harper, 1937. Free handling of sources; tendency to hero-worship renders many parts suspect. Undocumented.

SMITH, FRANK. *Thomas Paine: Liberator.* New York: Stokes, 1938. Best of the popular biographies; is clear, readable, and offers some new material. No documentation, bibliography, or index.

WILLIAMSON, AUDREY. *Thomas Paine: his Life, Work and Times.* London: George Allen & Unwin, Ltd., 1973. Very complete treatment of subject from a British point of view.

WOODWARD, W. E. *Tom Paine: America's Godfather.* New York: Dutton, 1945. Denies with monotonous repetition the various charges made against Paine through the years. Offers little in the way of interpetation.

2. Novels and Dramas

FAST, HOWARD. *Citizen Tom Paine.* New York: Duell, Sloan and Pearce, 1943. Vivid, fast-paced historical novel in which Paine emerges as a revolting yet compelling and appealing character, the first man to practice revolution as a sole reason for being. Eminently readable.

FOSTER, PAUL. *Tom Paine: A Play in Two Parts.* New York: Grove Press,1967. This highly inventive play utilizes improvisation, audience participation, telescoped time, stylized sets and action in order present the many facets of Paine's personality.

164                                                 THOMAS PAINE

3. Books

BRADFORD, GAMALIEL. *Damaged Souls.* Boston and New York: Hough-
ton Mifflin, 1922. Exploits the "rebel" motif. Sees Paine as an idealist who thought he could best accomplish his ends by destructive
rather than constructive means.
BROWNE, RAY B. *The Burke-Paine Controversy: Texts and Criticism.* New
York: Harcourt, Brace & World, 1963. Casebook format presents
abridgements of *Reflections* and *Rights,* contemporary reactions, and
twentieth-century criticism.
DISHMAN, ROBERT B. *Burke and Paine on Revolution and the Rights of
Man.* New York: Scribner's, 1971. Lengthy introduction offers excel-
lent background to the Paine-Burke controversy over the French
Revolution.
FENNESSY, R. R. *Burke, Paine and the Rights of Man.* The Hague:
Martinus Nijhoff, 1963. Explores the irreconcilable points of view
toward the French Revolution held by Paine and Burke.
FICHTER, JOSEPH H., S.J. *Roots of Change.* New York: D.
Appleton–Century, 1939. Considers Paine from the standpoint of his
importance in the history of the relationship between the classes of
society.
JOHNSON, GERALD WHITE. *The Lunatic Fringe.* New York: Lippincott,
1957. Uses Paine to illustrate thesis that the "lunatic fringe" must be
tolerated; that America must not resort to the use of legal or extra-
legal means to suppress unpopular opinions.
JONES, HOWARD MUMFORD. *Belief and Disbelief in American Literature.*
Chicago and London: University of Chicago Press, 1967. Views
Paine's religious writings as part of his effort to establish a new form
of faith, a republican religion.
MCCONNELL, FRANCIS J. *Evangelicals, Revolutionists and Idealists: Six
English Contributors to American Thought and Action.* New York:
Abingdon-Cokesbury, 1942. Modern Protestant theologian concludes
that Paine's theology was not so much false as inadequate. Some
worthwhile comments on *The Age of Reason.*
RUSTERHOLTZ, WALLACE P. *American Heretics and Saints.* Boston: Man-
thorne & Burack, 1938. Considers Paine's contributions to religious
liberalism and progressivism in America.
SMITH, T. V. "Thomas Paine: Voice of Democratic Revolution." *The
Philosophy of American Democracy.* Ed. Charner M. Perry.
Chicago: University of Chicago Press, 1943. Views Paine as a model
revolutionary. An acute analysis of his revolutionary philosophy by a
distinguished scholar.
SMITHLINE, ARNOLD. *Natural Religion in American Literature.* New
Haven, Conn.: College & University Press, 1966. Explicates *The Age*

*of Reason* in terms of its relationship to the history of natural religion in America. Valuable.

THOMAS, NORMAN. *Great Dissenters.* New York: Norton, 1961. Readable biographical account illustrates thesis that heresy has always been a creative force in society.

THOMPSON, IRA M., JR. *The Religions Views of Thomas Paine.* New York: Vantage Press, 1965. Published master's thesis compiles Paine's statements concerning religion; concludes that he was "the last outstanding advocate of the deistic movement."

4. Articles

ABEL, DARREL. "The Significance of the Letter to the Abbé Raynal in the Progress of Thomas Paine's Thought," *Pennsylvania Magazine of History and Biography,* LXVI (1942), 176–90. Views the letter as representing the stage in the progress of Paine's opinion where he actually ceased to think in nationalistic terms and became a practical internationalist.

ALDRIDGE, ALFRED OWEN. "The Poetry of Thomas Paine," *Pennsylvania Magazine of History and Biography,* LXXIX (1955), 81–99. Thorough review of Paine's poetry convinces Aldridge that some of it has sufficient merit to justify our attention to it as work of art.

———. "Thomas Paine and the Classics," *Eighteenth-Century Studies,* I (1968), 370–80. Finds Paine fundamentally antagonistic toward the Classics and uninspired by the Classical tradition.

BRESSLER, LEO A. "Peter Porcupine and the Bones of Thomas Paine," *Pennsylvania Magazine of History and Biography,* LXXXII (1958), 176–85. Full, readable, documented account of the part Cobbett played in the removal of Paine's bones.

CALVERTON, V. F. "Thomas Paine: God-Intoxicated Revolutionary." *Scribner's,* XCV (1934), 15–22. "Magazine biography" by a leading Marxist critic; depicts Paine as a revolutionary who saw the conflict between the old order and the new only in terms of its political perspective.

CLARK, HARRY HAYDEN. "An Historical Interpretation of Thomas Paine's Religion," *University of California Chronicle,* XXXV (1933), 56–87. Attributes the main premises of Paine's constructive religious thought to the influence of scientific Deism as put forward by the popularizers of Newtonianism.

———. "Toward a Reinterpretation of Thomas Paine," *American Literature,* V (1933–34), 133–45. While Quakerism helped to mold Paine's mind, scientific Deism and humanitarianism inspired his widely influential theories on religion, politics, economics, social service, literary composition. A good summary of several previously elaborated themes.

DORFMAN, JOSEPH. "The Economic Philosophy of Thomas Paine," *Political Science Quarterly*, LIII (1938), 372–86. Good general summary of Paine's economic theories as set forth in the principal works. Concludes that, as a whole, "they represent a scheme of things closely resembling that of the Benthamites a generation later."

FALK, ROBERT P. "Thomas Paine: Deist or Quaker?," *Pennsylvania Magazine of History and Biography*, LXII (1938), 52–63. Admits that Paine's zeal for humanitarian reform shows the Quaker influence but maintains that his essential creed was Deism. Fully documented and convincing.

KENYON, CECILIA M. "Where Paine Went Wrong," *American Political Science Review*, XLV (1951), 1086–99. States that it was Paine, not the American people, who failed to understand politics, and that this failure was the initial cause of his rejection by his fellow Americans.

KNUDSON, JERRY W. "The Rage Around Tom Paine: Newspaper Reactions to His Homecoming in 1802," *New York Historical Society Quarterly Bulletin*, LIII (1969), 34–63. Thorough detailing of the attack made on Paine by the Federalist press at his return to America. Views him as merely a pawn in a purely partisan issue.

LEFFMANN, HENRY. "The Real Thomas Paine, Patriot and Publicist. A Philosopher Misunderstood," *Pennsylvania Magazine of History and Biography*, XLVI (1922), 81–99. Labels *The Age of Reason* as responsible for Paine's being much misunderstood and cruelly abused, although he had the highest motives in writing it.

MATTHEWS, ALBERT "Thomas Paine and the Declaration of Independence," *Proceedings of the Massachusetts Historical Society*, XLIII (1910), 241–53. Attempts to prove through careful documentation that Conway's attribution to Paine of part of the drafting of the Declaration is unwarranted and that Jefferson is the sole author of the document.

MILLER, PERRY. "Thomas Paine, Rationalist," *Nation*, CLXII (1946), 228–32. Specifies Paine's usage of the language of an eighteenth-century rationalist as accountable for the decline of his popularity in the nineteenth century.

NICHOLSON, MARJORIE. "Thomas Paine, Edward Nares, and Mrs. Piozzi's Marginalia," *Huntington Library Bulletin*, No. 10 (1936), 103–33. Closely examines Reverend Nares's refutation of the "plurality of worlds" thesis as developed by Paine. Good discussion of the influence of science on Paine.

PENNIMAN, HOWARD. "Thomas Paine — Democrat," *American Political Science Review*, XXXVII (1943), 244–62. Reexamines Paine's political doctrines with respect to the following: popular sovereignty, majority rule, equality, popular consultation, democracy, and Deism.

PERSINGER, CLARK EDMUND. "The Political Philosophy of Thomas

Paine," University of Nebraska *Graduate Bulletin,* 7th Series (July 1901), 54-74. Establishes five general principles of revolutionary thought and employs them as a standard by which to measure Paine's philosophy. Presents Paine's political ideas by topical arrangement and without much comment or criticism.

PROCHASKA, FRANKLYN K. "Thomas Paine's *The Age of Reason* Revisited," *Journal of the History of Ideas,* XXXIII (1972), 561-76. Concludes that some of the commonly held assumptions about the *Age of Reason* controversy need revision.

SMITH, FRANK. *"New Light on Thomas Paine's First Year in America, 1775,"* *American Literature,* I (1929-30), 347-71. Establishes Paine as the author of twenty-seven pieces in 1775 and offers new evidence concerning the date of arrival in America and tenure with the *Pennsylvania Magazine.*

VANDERHAAR, MARGARET M. "Whitman, Paine, and the Religion of Democracy," *Walt Whitman Review* (March 16, 1970) 14-22. Shows that Paine and Whitman shared many religious, philosophical, and social ideas.

WECTER, DIXON. "Thomas Paine and the Franklins," *American Literature,* XII (1940-41), 306-17. Views the correspondence between Paine and Franklin as having substantial interest because of the fundamental difference in their attitudes as revolutionaries. Reprints three newly discovered letters and reviews other known correspondence.

# Index

168